THE
BROCKPORT MURDER
DOG TRIAL

THE BROCKPORT MURDER DOG TRIAL

Bizarre Tragedy and Spectacle on the Erie Canal

BILL HULLFISH & LAURIE FORTUNE VERBRIDGE

THE
History
PRESS

Published by The History Press
Charleston, SC
www.historypress.com

Front cover, top left: Grinberg Paramount Pathe Inc., used with permission; *top right*: author's collection; *bottom left*: Grinberg Paramount Pathe Inc., used with permission; *bottom right*: Grinberg Paramount Pathe Inc., used with permission.
Back cover, top left: Grinberg Paramount Pathe Inc., used with permission; *top right*: Grinberg Paramount Pathe Inc., used with permission; *bottom left*: Grinberg Paramount Pathe Inc., used with permission; *bottom right*: Grinberg Paramount Pathe Inc., used with permission.

First published 2021

Manufactured in the United States

ISBN 9781467148306

Library of Congress Control Number: 2020951663

In memory of Maxwell Breeze and his family and offered with sincere sympathy for the tragedy they endured.

This book is dedicated to Victor Fortune and the people of Brockport, to preserve the historical record of this event for generations to come.

CONTENTS

CONTENTS

FOREWORD

I've often sat along the banks of the Erie Canal at Brockport's summer music series and listened to William Hullfish and his band entertain the crowd with folk songs. When I needed a musician to play an appropriate instrument at the beginning of our local museum's event, Bill agreed to play his pennywhistle. His superb technique and the instrument's haunting sound harkened the audience back to a bargeman's lonely life and set the evening's tone. For me, Bill and music are inseparable.

Recently, Bill called to inform me that he was working on a new project—one that didn't involve music. As I was the lead volunteer at Brockport's Emily L. Knapp Museum of Local History, he asked if we had any information about a 1936 murder trial involving a dog named Idaho. I searched our collection and found one poster with a picture of Idaho and several unidentified people.

Later, he asked if I would write the foreword for this new book. I was honored but wanted to understand his sudden switch from one genre to another. Bill without a guitar, and murder instead of music, seemed a stretch.

Bill's musical aspirations began when his mother encouraged him to sing in the church choir and school music groups. Classical music and jazz became his passion and developed into his learning to play the saxophone, clarinet and a variety of other instruments. During the Vietnam War years, he fell in love with folk and protest music, further expanding his repertoire.

After completing high school in New Jersey, Bill's father encouraged him to become a music teacher. He entered Trenton State College (now the College of New Jersey).

Bill told me, "I didn't want to teach. I just wanted to play music."

He left college and auditioned for the U.S. Air Force Band. He was accepted because he could sing and play many instruments. As a member of the Singing Sergeants, he toured the United States and Canada in the spring and fall and continued to pursue a college degree at the University of Maryland. By the end of his six-year stay in the Air Force, Bill had finished his BS in music education and his master of music (MM) degree.

Sometimes in life, all the stars are in alignment. In 1964, SUNY Brockport, a college built near the historic Erie Canal, hired Bill to teach music. He taught everything from woodwind instruments and intro to music to folk music. Although married with a young family, with the help of the GI Bill, Bill obtained his doctorate degree.

In 1978, fate again played a role in his life. Most of the students in his folk music class played instruments, including dulcimer, pennywhistle and guitar. Others had excellent voices. It was the first time that had ever happened. The simplest way for Bill to teach them was to form a band, which morphed into the Golden Eagle String Band. The band, including two members of the 1978 class, continues to perform throughout the United States. Their recordings are in the Smithsonian Folkways Collection in Washington, D.C.

When he wasn't teaching, Bill collected folk music for an upcoming book and enjoyed reading newspaper articles about local history. That's when he first read about the dog murder trial. He wanted to know more about the bizarre story but was busy teaching, writing his book and raising a family, leaving him little time for research. Eventually, SUNY Brockport discontinued its music program and transferred him to the theater department. His colleague also knew about Idaho. Bill shared his information with her, and she turned the story into a children's play called *The Shaggy Dog Murder Trial*.

Until Bill retired, the dog story percolated in the back of his mind, but he didn't pursue it until the internet became available, giving him access to a world of information. He read newspaper articles from all over the country and realized the Idaho murder trial had captured the nation's attention. Major papers, including the *New York Times* and *Chicago Tribune*, had descended on Brockport with their reporters. Film crews also arrived. So many came, in fact, that the trial was moved to a larger facility.

His son, a film editor, became involved in the project. He had connections to Paramount Picture's archives and learned that a film clip of the trial existed. Although it required splicing and restoration, his son was able to restore that short piece of Brockport history into a pristine film, which includes the trial's major participants.

Social media provided the final piece of the puzzle when Bill broadcast a request for information about the trial. Laurie Verbridge, the daughter of Idaho's owner, Victor Fortune, contacted him. For years, she had interviewed her father and kept notes of his version of the trial in hopes of someday writing a story.

To have firsthand knowledge from a participant in the trial was more than Bill could have hoped for. There was no turning back. They agreed to cowrite a book.

Bill had found his next book—not about music, but about an incident from Brockport's history that begged to be told. And Laurie could finally tell a family story she had learned about in a manner she would never forget.

Sue Savard
Emily Knapp Museum, Brockport, New York

PREFACE

My first day of fourth grade at Marion Central School in Upstate New York was exciting. My grandmother Fortune found me a special dress from her neighbor's children, and I went to school feeling pretty optimistic about that year. My classroom was across the hall from the new principal's office.

The announcements came over the loudspeaker, and we were getting acquainted with our new teacher, Mr. Dunham. There was a knock on the door, and I was asked by an office worker to come to the principal's office. Mr. Dunham excused me, and I left the room.

I had never been to the principal's office before and was sitting on a green chair with metal around it, swinging my feet, when Principal Green came up to me and asked me to come into his office. I remember feeling a little bit nervous when he began speaking in a firm voice.

"Are you Victor Fortune's daughter?"

I replied, "Yes."

"Was your father from Brockport, New York?"

I said, "That's where my Grandma and Grandpa Fortune live, but he was born in Medina, New York."

Principal Green asked in a deep voice, "Did you know that your father had a dog named Idaho?"

I said, "No."

Mr. Green went on. "Well, your father had a dog named Idaho. That dog used to swim in the Brockport canal. Your father's dog murdered one of my best friends by drowning him in the canal. You need to go home and ask your father about that. You can return to your classroom now."

I remember being baffled by the statement. I felt like I was in trouble but didn't know why. I don't really think I knew much about murder or drowning, but I went through the day and went home and told my dad. He became very upset and said it was not quite like Principal Green said. We would talk about it later.

The next day, my two sisters and I did not go to school. Dad and Mom didn't go to work, either. They sat my two sisters and me down on the sofa, and we learned the story of my father's dog Idaho.

—Laurie Fortune Verbridge

Unlike Laurie, my introduction to Idaho came forty years ago, when I first came upon an obscure reference to the Brockport murder dog trial. I was curious and went to find a copy of the trial transcript at the Village of Brockport Court. I learned that the court did not keep trial transcripts after a certain number of years. Judge Homer B. Benedict retired to Florida in 1937, only a year after he had presided over this case, and he took his court records with him. I was given his address, and I wrote to Homer Benedict, asking for a copy of the transcript. I soon received a letter from his son saying that, after his father died in 1947, the family discarded the old court records. It was then that I carefully read an article in the *New York Times* stating that the trial had actually been held in the town of Sweden Court. I called there and, after a few days, was informed that the transcript had been destroyed.

Not to be deterred, I started searching the newspapers known to have sent reporters to Brockport for the trial. From some of these sources, I pieced together an ad hoc transcript and eventually abandoned my research due to lack of time. One of my colleagues in the theater department at SUNY College at Brockport was interested in the case, and I gave her my research. She subsequently wrote a play for children based loosely on the subject.

Well, here it is, all these years later. I am now retired, have lived in Brockport for fifty-seven years and am more interested in local history than ever. I started going over my old notes and doing more digging through old newspapers, helped now by the internet. Through my son, Steve, a film editor, I was able to obtain the 1936 newsreel and cue sheet from Paramount News's\ "The Eyes and Ears of the World," taken at the Brockport trial, and the film *Killer-Dog*, an MGM short subject produced in August 1936 to take advantage of publicity from the Brockport Murder Dog Trial. This put faces and voices to people in the past who were part of my search into this fascinating event. Through social media, unavailable when I started forty years ago, I was able to meet with Laurie Verbridge, the daughter of Victor Fortune, the central character in this story. She was also writing a book on the Brockport trial based on interviews with her father. Now things were really coming together. After all these years, reading old newspaper articles and piecing together parts of this story, I was about to hear the words of an eyewitness to this event. And not just any eyewitness. Laurie had the words of her father, Victor, owner of the dog Idaho, dubbed by the media as the "Murder Dog."

Laurie and I decided to share our information and become coauthors. We added the information provided by Laurie's interviews with her father and his documents and family photos. We then combined that with new information from searching hundreds of internet sources, listening to actual participants in the murder trial on the Paramount newsreel and visiting the Brockport museum, libraries and local cemeteries.

When I first became interested in this story, forty years ago, Victor Fortune and many of the other people involved in this trial were still alive, but I missed my chance. Laurie informed me that the youngest eyewitness, Jack Fortune, who would now be ninety-four years old, had died. Despite these setbacks, it was still worth gathering everything we had and putting the story together. I now had information I might not have been able to gather back in the 1980s. My son became a film editor and had many contacts with the right people for obtaining and editing films from the event's era. He located a source for the Paramount newsreel taken in Brockport. He also located the *Killer-Dog* film from 1936.

As it turns out, the newsreel took some time and effort to locate, even by the archivists at Paramount. The first response to our inquiry about the 1936 newsreel was that they could not find it. Then, a few days later, they came up with good and bad news. The good news was that they found the newsreel. The bad news was that it had never been digitized and the old acetate film was in very fragile condition and needed to be spliced back together in a number of places. They agreed, for a small fee, to do the work and send us a copy. My son spent many hours editing the film to make it clearer, remove duplicate footage and return the newsreel to its original order.

Then, we were able to obtain prints of individual frames of all the participants in the trial. Family photos, if we could get them, would show the people in the trial at different ages. We now had actual photographs of the participants on the day of the trial. For another reasonable fee, we obtained the rights to show the newsreel and print the still-frame photographs.

Obtaining a copy of the other 1936 film, *Killer-Dog*, was a bit easier, since the restoration of the short-subject film was already done and a DVD of it was available from Turner Classic Films. Rights to use the film and the still frame images proved to be beyond our means, but I was able to obtain information about the film from the International Movie Database and the one surviving member of the cast, who was five years old in 1936.

The references to the Civilian Conservation Corps (CCC) and the Works Progress Administration (WPA) are reminders that this happened during the Great Depression. Both Victor Fortune and his father, George, had jobs through the New Deal work projects. George Fortune, William Breeze, father of the boy who drowned; and other Brockport men were employed by the WPA. Victor worked for two years in the CCC. The description by Victor Fortune of his life in the CCC and his moving story of how the Great Depression affected his family provide insight into how the Depression affected similar families.

And, so it is, after years of interviews and research, we have finally pieced together everything into this book. Since the original trial transcript does not exist, we cannot guarantee that the trial took place in this exact order or that no witnesses have been left out, but this is an accurate account of what has been reported on the subject. In addition, we used information from the original court document that served as a "summons" or "notice" to Victor Fortune. No dialogue or testimony has been fabricated. This story is stranger than fiction. No one could concoct anything this bizarre. However, the Village of Brockport got its fifteen minutes of fame.

—Bill Hullfish

ACKNOWLEDGEMENTS

Bill: Thanks to Steve and Brian Hullfish, who connected me with Laurie Fortune Verbridge, someone I probably would never have found without their social media skills. Then Steve, with his film editing contacts, found the Paramount newsreel of the Brockport trial and was able to have it transferred to a lab to have the original acetate film spliced back together and digitized. Steve was able to edit the footage and pull out the individual still-frame photographs. Without these crucial elements, this book would not have been possible. Thank you to Sue Savard for research, documents and photographs from the Emily Knapp Museum and for writing the foreword for this book.

Laurie: Special thanks to Tim Ryan of the Seymour Library, for his research and copies of documents from the Local History section; Lynnette Cox of the First Baptist Church in Brockport, membership chair, for researching information on the Breeze family; Tim Dolan, for putting me in touch with Steve and Bill Hullfish; and Jim Fallon, acting superintendent of Brockport Central Schools, for trying to locate a picture of Maxwell. Thanks to Karl Green, principal of Marion Central Schools, whose statements made an impact on me and gave me the desire to tell the story of Idaho; Emily Verbridge Decker, my daughter, for editing, rewriting and encouragement; Victor Fortune, my father, for his story; Lynne Fortune DeLyser, my sister, for encouragement, for reading all of Dad's notes and for making sure they were accurate; Michael and Patrick

Verbridge, for support, for reading the story and for making suggestions; Tom Sonneville, for encouragement and making life simple during the research and writing; and Paula Warr, member of the Breeze family, for researching family information on Maxwell and his family.

1
PRELUDE TO TRAGEDY

The *New York Times* declared the Brockport murder trial "equal to any murder trial in the country."[1] One journalist wrote that it had "all the trappings of a Bruno Hauptmann trial,"[2] referring to the man charged with kidnapping Charles Lindbergh's baby. Another reporter called it "one of the most unusual death penalty cases ever."[3] A columnist described it as "one of the oddest trials on record."[4] A playwright declared that her dramatization "is based on one of America's most unusual court cases."[5]

Paramount Pictures dispatched its "The Eyes and Ears of the World" news crew. Hundreds of newspapers from coast to coast carried headlines of the trial. The Associated Press (AP) and reporters and photographers from major news organizations from across the country arrived to cover the trial. The story spread far and wide, all over America. Every newspaper printed long accounts of it. There were editorials both pro and con.

Twenty-seven witnesses were called. A look-alike was brought in to cast doubt on the eyewitness identification of the murder suspect. A two-week delay in the trial was ordered so that the accused perpetrator could be evaluated. A national expert was contacted to examine the alleged murderer. The trial was moved to accommodate the expected crowd of up to five hundred people. And, at the center of all that attention, was a dog named Idaho who, according to one journalist, was "for a time the most talked-of dog on earth."[6] Author and nationally syndicated dog columnist Albert Payson Terhune called it "the most spectacular case involving a dog in the history of criminal law."[7]

Brockport Main Street Erie Canal Bridge. *Photograph brockportny.org.*

Newspapers from Rochester, New York's *Democrat and Chronicle* to the *New York Times*, the *Chicago Tribune* and the *Tyler Morning Telegraph* of Tyler, Texas, ran headlines like these:

> *Brockport Tragedy Led to Trial for Murder*
> *Puppy Goes on Trial for His Life Today*
> *Pup on Trial for Life Snores While Witnesses Testify*
> *Idaho, Mongrel Dog, Goes on Trial for Life in Drowning of Youth*
> *Idaho Charged with Causing Boy, Fourteen, to Drown*

Terhune, who was requested as an expert witness for the trial, eventually wrote a detailed account of Idaho and the Brockport "murder dog" trial. Here, he presents his reason for including Idaho in his "Tales of Real Dogs": "When metropolitan newspapers devote from two to three columns of space, each, on a busy day, to the court trial of a dog and when they make that trial a front page feature and when they lead up to the case with a dozen preliminary accounts and editorial mention—well, the whole thing must constitute a mighty good dog story."[8]

What was it about the Brockport "murder dog" trial that attracted all of this attention? It started innocently, when a group of boys went out on a hot July 4 in 1936 to play baseball. They were part of a team called the Muckland Nine, made up of boys who lived north of the Erie Canal in the Village of Brockport, New York: Max Breeze, Donald Duff, Paul Hamlin, George Glynn, Bernard Brule, Beverly Fogg, Joseph Keable, E. Eisenberg and Kearney.[9] The Mucklanders played in a youth league at Webaco Field on Holley Street in Brockport. They had opened the season back in April with an exciting game in which fifty-one runs were scored. The Muckland Nine scored twenty-five runs; unfortunately, the other team scored twenty-six.[10]

In a reminiscence from the files of the Emily L. Knapp Local History Museum, Phyllis Schafer describes the youth recreation situation in Brockport in 1936:

> *The year was 1936, the month, July, and the location, the Village of Brockport. The village was smaller than we know it today. There were no public playgrounds. There were two public schools, a Parochial school, and the Normal School. The high school was completed in 1934. The campus of this school had not yet been developed as a playground for out-of-school hours. Boys and girls tended to find vacant lots for their games of baseball. The high school was not yet in the pattern of play.*
>
> *Swimming pools just did not exist as they do today. Children who wanted to swim had to go to the lake. That was not always easy. Some boys would go to the quarries out on canal road. Then there were others who swam in the Barge Canal. It was not unusual to see a group of boys diving from the gates by the west bridge. The waters of the canal were deep and among other things terribly polluted. However, it was convenient, a temptation, and seemed to be a good place to cool off on a warm day.[11]*

The Barge Canal to which Phyllis Schafer refers is the Erie Canal; some locals called it the Brockport Canal. In 1905, the State of New York started construction to modernize its canals into the Barge Canal System. Each canal (the Erie, the Oswego, the Cayuga/Seneca and the Champlain) kept its individual name. It is common for people to refer to the canal that runs through Brockport as the Barge Canal, the Erie Canal or the Brockport Canal.

The place where the boys swam, as described by Schafer, is the guard gate just west of the bridge, sometimes referred to as the Third Bridge, the High Bridge or Smith Street Bridge. The Village of Brockport has three bridges over the canal within the village limits; the easternmost bridge, or the Park Avenue Lift Bridge; the Main Street Lift Bridge; and the westernmost bridge or, if you are headed west on the canal, the Third Bridge. The first two bridges are lift bridges, but the third bridge is often called the High Bridge, because it is a fixed bridge, constructed high enough for boats to pass under it.

Phyllis Schafer continues her account of events on that fateful day: "On July 4, 1936, a group of boys had been playing at the Webaco baseball field. This was, as I remember it, an open field next to the Webaco oil tanks out Holley Street. At this time Holley Street was not developed at the west end and there was much open land."[12]

Even for current residents of Brockport, a bit of explanation might help here. According to local newspaper accounts, by 1935, Webaco Field was not just an open field. It was a ballpark that included seating for spectators and was lit so that night events could be held there. Everything from adult and youth baseball and softball league games to donkey baseball and band and chorus concerts were held at Webaco Field.[13] The field was named after the Webster Oil Company, which had branches all around Monroe County, including one on Holley Street in Brockport.

After the game, Maxie Breeze and some of the Muckland Nine began to walk down the south bank of the Erie Canal toward the center of the Village of Brockport. A dog started to follow them. Approaching the bridge west of the Main Street lift bridge, often called "Third Bridge," they decided to cool off with a swim in the canal. This spot offered a bit of privacy and a cement wall so that swimmers did not have to scramble over sharp rocks.

Max was splashing in the water when the dog that followed them from Webaco Field jumped in and started to interfere with Max's ability to swim. Max struggled to free himself from the dog and paddled even farther out in the canal, trying to get away. Then, Max had trouble swimming, started to panic and began to call for help. A teammate from the Muckland Nine, Paul Hamlin, sixteen, swam over to help Max and soon found himself fighting off the dog. Hamlin started to help Max toward the canal bank when the dog latched onto Paul. As he struggled to shake the dog off, Paul lost his grip on Max, who went under in the murky water. Paul hollered to the other boys on the canal bank to get help. Donald Duff ran to an adjacent street and attracted the attention of Brockport Police deputy James Costigan, who called for the fire rescue crew. Max had completely disappeared in the water, and it took the fire rescue crew, using grappling hooks, to bring his body to the surface. The coroner, who had also been called by the deputy, pronounced Max dead. The police were dispatched to tell Max's parents that their only son had drowned in the Erie Canal.[14]

Victor Fortune, twenty-five, was the owner of the dog, Idaho, identified by the boys as the dog in the canal. Fortune describes where he was and what he was doing on that fateful July 4:

Path along canal leading to the Third Bridge. *Photograph by Stephen Hullfish.*

The Third Bridge. *Photograph by Stephen Hullfish.*

July 4, 1936: The gang was all getting together at Hamlin Beach State Park in the afternoon. Idaho and I took a walk and swim early in the morning. During that time, firecrackers were going off and he was scared to death.

When we returned home, he went to our room and got under the bed. He was petrified. I decided I should leave him home with Mom and Dad.

I took off for the picnic. My folks were sitting on the porch as it was already extremely hot. Idaho had joined them, and Mom said she'd keep an eye on him if the firecrackers and fireworks got loud. I planned to be home before nightfall because I knew Idaho would have a tough time. I could see the kids playing in the neighborhood ballfield laughing and enjoying their day. It was really a hot, sunny day.[15]

It was not long before the police and Maxwell Breeze's parents learned that a dog identified as "Idaho" was involved with Max's death. The police visited the Fortune home and demanded that Idaho be confined until a hearing could be held to determine if the dog was dangerous. The Fortune family insisted that Idaho was home with them and could not have been the dog in the canal with Maxwell. Almost a week went by. Just when Victor thought things could not get worse, they did. Idaho was accused of attacking another swimmer in the Erie Canal. Victor Fortune describes the events that followed.

Following the tragedy, there were several more attacks on swimmers at third bridge. I had taken Idaho swimming but had been with him every moment during that time period. He was always under my watch and never went alone. I kept him leashed except when swimming. In spite of this, Daniel Houghton, 21, was sure that the dog doing this was Idaho. He filed a complaint on a dangerous dog, identified as Idaho, on July 17, 1936 with Constable George and we were to report to Justice Benedict's office on Tuesday, July 21 at 1:00 p.m. The complaint stated that the dog Idaho was dangerous and that on July 11 and July 13, when Daniel Houghton was swimming, Idaho attacked him by climbing on his back. Daniel stated that Idaho was a vicious dog. The hearing on the 17th [sic] was solely based on Daniel's charges but it opened up Max's tragic drowning.[16]

In the meantime, Maxie Breeze's funeral took place on July 7 at 2:30 p.m. at the Breeze home on East Avenue in the Village of Brockport. From there, mourners gathered at Lakeview Cemetery. Even though Max was

Victor Fortune swimming with Idaho. *Photograph from author's collection.*

an only child, his mother came from a large local family. Mr. and Mrs. Alonzo Wilson had ten children, and by the time the youngest was born, his older siblings were already married and had families of their own. Max's uncle Jack Wilson was born the same year as Max, 1924. Also attending the service at Lakeview Cemetery were Max's friends from his family's affiliation with the Baptist Church, members of his Boy Scout troop, schoolmates and teammates. In all, about one hundred mourners gathered on a grassy knoll south of Brockport for the burial service of Russell Maxwell Breeze.[17]

Victor Fortune was familiar with Max and his family. He said Max was devoted to his mother who, as an invalid, used a wheelchair to get around.

> *Maxwell Breeze was a really nice kid and his parents were nice people. His Dad William had immigrated to the United States from Canada when Max was about a year old. His Mom Anna was born in Rochester NY and married Willie in Toronto Canada. His Dad worked for the WPA just like my Dad. They had really struggled through the Great Depression. Max was only 14 and their only son.*[18]

25

Maxwell Breeze's grave in Lakeview Cemetery, Brockport, New York. *Photograph by the author.*

Maxwell Breeze was a well-liked and active member of many groups. The day of the drowning, he was playing baseball with the Muckland Nine, a team that practiced and played numerous games together in a youth league. Max was also active with the Boy Scouts, earning many awards and merit badges, and he participated in overnight camping trips with his troop. He participated in school activities as a singer and actor in school dramatic productions.[19]

After this, the village divided into two factions: one believed that Victor Fortune's dog was responsible for Max's drowning and should be killed; the other believed that Idaho was not responsible and should be freed. This division soon hit home for the Fortunes. Idaho received death threats, and the family was harassed. Victor describes the effect on his mother: "Community members and former friends were often confrontational, stating that Idaho should be put to death. Mom got so she didn't want to leave the house or even to go to Church. Idaho's life had been threatened more than once so we didn't let him leave our sight."[20]

Although Ada Fortune had a difficult time with the division in the community, Victor was confronted with the real possibility of losing Idaho, not only by someone taking the law into his own hands but also via a court-ordered death sentence. After the July 17 court summons, he had his first meeting with a representative from the Rochester Dog Protective Association and its veterinarian, William Mahoney. Victor had to deal with preparations for the July 21 hearing.

Idaho in cage. *Grinberg Paramount Pathe Inc., used with permission.*

Mary Foubister, a dog expert from Rochester Dog Protective Association came to visit me and meet Idaho right after I received the notice to appear at the July 21st hearing. We had a long talk. She was concerned that someone was going to try to hurt Idaho. She suggested I voluntarily turn him over to the protective agency. I decided that would be the best thing to do with all the accusations in the village and took him to the association kennel on Scottsville Road the day before we were to go to the hearing [July 21]. When they took Idaho, Mary was very nice but when she closed that kennel door, I felt such grief. I wondered if Idaho would ever come home again. Dr. Mahoney said not to worry, but I could not help but be worried.[21]

Victor had good reason to worry. Would a hearing in the law office of Justice Homer B. Benedict be his only chance to defend Idaho from a death sentence? Mary and Dr. Mahoney were not even listed as witnesses for the hearing. Would they be given a chance to speak in Idaho's defense? What would the hearing decide?

2
AN UNUSUAL HEARING

On a hot July 21, in the crowded second-floor law office of Judge Homer B. Benedict at 37 Main Street in the Village of Brockport, a preliminary hearing was held. Reporters, photographers, witnesses and spectators filled the office. Judge Benedict began the proceedings, under New York's Agriculture and Markets Law (Chapter 69 of the Consolidated Laws, Article 7, §12: Dangerous dogs), by reading the articles that applied to the hearing.

> *Any person who witnesses an attack or threatened attack, or in the case of a minor, an adult acting on behalf of such minor, may, and any dog control officer or police officer as provided in subdivision one of this section shall, make a complaint under oath or affirmation to any municipal judge or justice of such attack or threatened attack. Thereupon, the judge or justice shall immediately determine if there is probable cause to believe the dog is a dangerous dog and, if so, shall issue an order to any dog control officer, peace officer, acting pursuant to his or her special duties, or police officer directing such officer to immediately seize such dog and hold the same pending judicial determination as provided in this section. Whether or not the judge or justice finds there is probable cause for such seizure, he or she shall, within five days and upon written notice of not less than two days to the owner of the dog, hold a hearing on the complaint. The petitioner shall have the burden at such hearing to prove the dog is a "dangerous dog" by clear and convincing evidence.*

Homer Benedict Law Office (*second floor of store next to the large corner building*). *Author's collection.*

Justice Benedict followed the letter of the law in calling the hearing. Immediately after Daniel Houghton's complaint arrived on his desk, Benedict had the "notice" served to Victor Fortune on July 17. The hearing was held on July 21, within the five-day period specified in the law, and giving the owner at least two days' notice. At the hearing, witnesses for the plaintiff (Daniel Houghton) were Donald Duff, Paul Hamlin, Daniel Houghton, James Costigan and Gene Hosmer. Witnesses for the defendant (Victor Fortune) were Victor Fortune, George Fortune and Arthur Merritt. During testimony at the hearing on July 21, friends of Max Breeze each identified Idaho as the dog that jumped on his back and caused him to drown. Victor Fortune describes what happened next:

> At that point I represented Idaho. Paul Hamlin who attempted to rescue Max when the dog climbed on his back, described Idaho as a great big black dog. Donald Duff, another friend of Max's, identified Idaho as the dog that followed him from the baseball field to the canal. Daniel Houghton, the petitioner, pressed for the dog's destruction as a vicious dog, based on two occasions he claimed Idaho attacked him in the water.

Justice Benedict directed the following questions to Donald Duff:

Q. What did the dog do to Max?

A. Just tried to climb on Max's back.

Q. Was Max playing with the dog before he went in the water?

A. No.

Q. What did Max do?

A. He got frightened and swam out toward the middle and hollered "The dog's after me. Help."

Q. What happened then?

A. Paul Hamlin swam out to help but the dog tried to climb on him and when he tried to shake him off, Max went down and Paul couldn't get him.[22]

George Fortune, Victor's father, testified that Idaho was with him on the porch the whole time and was still there when he heard the ambulance respond to the canal. Twenty-one-year-old Daniel Houghton claimed the dog had attacked him on two different occasions as he swam in the canal. Victor Fortune, the dog's owner, insisted that Idaho was simply playing around and wouldn't cause any harm. Arthur Merritt, a witness for Victor Fortune, testified that Daniel Houghton told him that he and his companions kept the dog in the water and the animal climbed on Daniel when it became tired.[23]

At this point, Mary Foubister, secretary of the Rochester Dog Protective Association, asked if she could take the stand. She had been caring for Idaho at the Scottsville shelter since shortly after the notice to appear was served. Even though she was not originally on the list of witnesses for the defense, Judge Benedict allowed her to speak to the court.

Mary stated, "Idaho is leading the plea for his life and liberty."[24]

Victor goes on to tell what happened in the hearing after Justice Benedict allowed Mary and veterinarian Dr. William Mahoney to testify.

Justice Benedict listened with some attention to the testimony of Dr. Mahoney regarding "Idaho" whom he had in his charge less than 24 hours. At Mary's request, I brought "Idaho" to the Association voluntarily late Monday and the hearing was on Wednesday.

"In this short time have you formed any opinion of his disposition?" asked Justice Benedict.

"He is playful and full of spirits like any normal pup," Mahoney replied.

"Would you consider him a dangerous dog?," Victor interjected.

"No, I certainly would not," answered the veterinarian.[25]

Mary Foubister said that New York State law required that an animal be observed by a veterinarian for a two-week period before it was adjudged to be vicious. The trial was postponed by Judge Benedict until August 5, 1936, so that the Rochester Dog Protective Association could continue to evaluate Idaho as to his demeanor on land and in the water. Idaho would continue to stay at the dog shelter and under protective custody. Dr. William H. Mahoney was charged with studying Idaho's "criminal tendencies."[26]

With the hearing over and the trial set for August 5, what more could be said? Well, the media had plenty to say. It was at this point that the news media began to muddy the waters. Immediately after the hearing on July 21, the Associated Press published a headline, picked up by newspapers all across the country, that Idaho was not present at his own hearing. The headline read "Master Hides Dog Facing Murder Trial," and the article went on to say, "A murder trial with no defendant present was the unique situation for Peace Justice Homer B. Benedict today as he convened a hearing to settle the fate of Idaho a half-grown dog accused of being responsible for the drowning of a high school boy."[27]

It is here that some confusion on the part of the press and Victor Fortune's description of what happened occurs. Victor was served with a notice (the word *summons* is crossed out on the document and *notice* written in) on July 17 to appear before Judge Benedict on July 21, along with witnesses (see court notice in appendix 3). At one point, Victor claims that Mary Foubister came to see him after the "hearing" on July 17. However, the July 17 date was when he was served with the notice to appear, not a hearing. Victor goes on to say that Mary talked him into giving Idaho up to her for the dog's own protection. It seems obvious that this occurred after Victor was served with the notice to appear and Mary made the decision not to bring Idaho to the July 21 hearing, knowing that Judge Benedict had the legal right to seize the dog.[28] Other accounts about the "notice" and the "hearing" were also confused. One report gave the dates of two hearings: one on July 17, and the other on July 19.[29] Mary's concern over Idaho being seized was well founded, because the law reads as follows: "If there was probable cause to believe the dog was a dangerous dog and, if so, could issue an order to any dog control officer, peace officer, acting pursuant to his or her special duties, or police officer directing such officer to immediately seize such dog and hold the same pending judicial determination as provided in this section."[30]

Was Mary Foubister protecting Idaho from being seized by not bringing him to the hearing and having the dog held by the Rochester Dog Protective

Association in Scottsville? It appears that Mary brought Dr. William Mahoney to the hearing knowing that the judge could not make a decision until Idaho was examined by a veterinarian and with the express purpose of having Mahoney do the examination for the court. If this was her plan, it worked perfectly, giving them time to prepare Idaho's defense and ensuring that Mahoney would be the veterinarian to assess Idaho's disposition on land and in the water. Mary knew the law and devised a very clever plan. She had probably done this before in other cases.

The media, not understanding that Victor, not Idaho, was the defendant summoned to the hearing, jumped on the story that the dog was missing. The defendant in this case, at the July 21 hearing, was Victor Fortune, who had the burden of proof in defending his dog against the charge that he was dangerous. A reading of the "notice" that Victor was served with on July 17 will clarify who was expected to attend the July 21 hearing.

> *Justice Court Civil Docket*
> *Trial Without Jury*
> *State of New York, County of Monroe*
> *Justice Court in Town of Sweden*
> *In the matter of the complaint of Daniel Houghton against an alleged Dangerous dog owned by Victor Fortune before Homer B. Benedict.*
> *July 17, 1936 notice* ["Summons" is crossed out and "Notice" is written in] *issued with complaint attached*
> *Notice returnable at one p.m. July 21st*
> *July 17, 1936 notice returned, personally served by George Hosmer, Constable.*
> *July 21, 1936 Case called at 1 p.m.*
> *Plaintiff, Daniel Houghton, appeared in person*
> *Plaintiff complained as follows: That Victor Fortune is the owner and harborer of a dangerous dog and the said dog, without just cause or provocation, did attack complainant while he was swimming in the Barge Canal by starting to climb on his back pushing him under the water, clawing and scratching him.*
> *Defendant answered as follows:*
> *Donald Duff, Paul Hamlin, Daniel Houghton, James Costigan and George Hosmer were sworn and testified for the complainant.*
> *Arthur Merritt, George Fortune, and Victor Fortune were sworn and testified for the defendant.*

Dr. William H. Mahoney, Mary Foubister were sworn and testified for defendant at request of Mary Foubister Executive Secretary of the Rochester Dog Protective Association. Defendant, Victor Fortune, appeared in person Case was adjourned to August 5, 1931 at 10 a.m.[31]

Neither Mary Foubister nor Dr. Mahoney were on the original notice but were allowed to be sworn in and testify at the hearing. Foubister bought them the time from July 21 to August 5 to raise money, hire a lawyer and prepare a defense. But even before the trial began, what should have been a simple, straightforward process was turning into the exact opposite. What kind of a trial did this portend?

3

EXTRAORDINARY PREPARATIONS

The two weeks between the hearing and the trial were filled with activity, on the part of both the defense and the media. Victor Fortune describes what happened after the hearing on the twenty-first:

Following the hearing on July 21ˢᵗ, I visited Idaho daily and began talking with Mary Foubister and she turned out to be a great friend to Idaho and me. "Vic," she said. "Idaho needs an attorney. I know you have no money, but I am sure we can raise enough to pay for one. Idaho has become pretty famous and I have spoken to Harry Sessions, a local attorney and animal lover. He is willing to take the case." I was speechless and although a man doesn't cry, I was fighting back tears of relief. I simply replied, "Thank you. I'll do whatever it takes. Idaho is innocent of all allegations." Mary called Mr. Sessions. We would meet the next day at the shelter office.

Mr. Sessions and Mary were in her office talking when I arrived. I was a little nervous. Mr. Sessions was a big personality and just a really great guy! He put me at ease right away. Mary brought Idaho into the office and he was all over me barking and nuzzling. Harry immediately said, "So this is our vicious dog?" I replied, "Yes Sir. This is Idaho!" Harry rubbed him, held his leash, and walked him outside while we talked. When we finished, he had interviewed both Idaho and me. Harry vowed he would save Idaho's life. For the first time since Max passed, I felt some relief and believed Idaho would have a chance of being found innocent. Additionally, Harry said that he had been following the case in the newspapers. He asked if I

Harry Sessions meets Idaho. *Reproduced by the author.*

knew that it had made national news and was showing up in worldwide news. I knew it was in lots of newspapers but had no idea that it had gone beyond New York State. Harry said, "Idaho has become a celebrity. We can also use that for his defense." I said, "Whatever it takes."

Mary went to work to raise the money. Within three days the call to help defend Idaho came out in the Democrat and Chronicle and the fund raising had begun. The headlines were: "Defense Fund Begun by Girl to Save Dog." The article concluded with: "Miss Marjorie Boyce, 21 of Thayer Street began the 'Idaho Defense Fund' to raise enough money for Victor Fortune to procure legal services."[32]

It was during this two-week recess, from July 21 to August 5, that the story of the Brockport "murder dog" trial began to spread through the media like wildfire. Letters began to pour in, as well as donations for Idaho's defense. Harry A. Sessions, a prominent Rochester, New York attorney, agreed to defend Idaho. He began preparing his case just as if he were defending a person facing the death penalty.

Sessions sought out and subpoenaed more than thirty witnesses, contacted local and national authorities on dog behavior, located a look-alike dog to produce in court to test eyewitness identification, developed strategies for

35

cross-examination of the witnesses, raised objections to a local newspaper poll and even demanded that the dog be able to defend himself. "I don't see how in fairness the court can turn down my request,"[33] Sessions said.

As the national media spread the news of the trial across the country, letters and telegrams began to pour in to Judge Benedict's office from almost every state in the United States and even from Germany. Some were short and to the point.

Tie the dog up, don't shoot him.

Route 4, Box-45-R
Stockton, California
July 23rd, 1936.[34]

Other letters expressed the same opinion but were more explicit. This next letter brings up an important and overlooked point in the proceedings. It seems obvious that in the week following the drowning, when no charges were filed and no hearings were scheduled, that the drowning was being considered an accident. It was not until a complaint was filed by Daniel Houghton that the court became involved.

Justice of the Peace,
Homer Benedict
Dear Sir:
I have been reading in the Stockton Record about the little murder dog. I don't see how you can call the dog a murder dog. If it had been a human being that done it, you would have called it an accident. A poor little dumb animal that was taught to swim. I think it is a shame to kill it.
    I do hope that the next item I read is where you had freed the little Murder dog.
Truly,
Mrs. M. Wilkinson, Atlantic City, N.J.[35]

A communication with no street address was reported to have come from a Mrs. A.J. Illison of Rochester. The Rochester *Democrat and Chronicle* reported that she was not listed in the city directory or at the Rochester post office. Mrs. Illison wrote to say that she, her husband and two children witnessed the accident and that Idaho was pushed into the water by the boys. "I hope this innocent, playful puppy will be spared, for after all a dog is man's best friend." Her statement could not be substantiated in as much as she could not be located, and the swimming hole where she claimed to see the boys was not visible to a passerby.[36]

As Sessions expanded his search for witnesses, he sent a telegram to a well-known expert on dogs, Albert Payson Terhune, who published a newspaper column about dogs, "Tales of Real Dogs"; wrote features about dogs in the *Saturday Evening Post*, *Atlantic Monthly*, *Red Book* and *Ladies' Home Journal;* and was author of more than thirty books about dogs. Terhune was credited as the world's most prolific and successful writer of dog stories (*Lad: A Dog*, *Buff: A Collie* and others). Lad is said to be the model for the movie star Lassie. The phrase "shaggy dog story" is said to have originated with Terhune's writings. He was known to devote eleven hours a day, six days a week for some thirty years to writing. His kennels, Sunnybank, became the most famed collie kennels in the nation.[37] The telegram mentioned at the start of this paragraph, which Sessions sent to Terhune, read as follows:

> *I am preparing the defense of Idaho, a nine-month-old Airedale-Shepherd dog, on trial for his life before Justice Homer Benedict at Village Hall, Brockport, N.Y., on Aug. 5 at 10 o'clock. Dog lovers and societies throughout the country are interested in this trial. I would like you to examine the dog as to his traits in the water and testify from your own recognized experience.*[38]

Sessions did not receive an immediate reply, but Terhune, who was interviewed about the Brockport trial by several news organizations, finally contacted him with advice on how to proceed in Idaho's defense. Terhune saw no reason why he would need to personally examine Idaho or appear in court.

> *There was no need for me to examine the puppy, in order to learn about his traits in the water. I knew well, from experience, what those traits must be; even though I never had set eyes on Idaho. I explained them and my own opinion of the case, at some length, to Mr. Sessions as well as to representatives of several newspapers and news associations which interviewed me on the subject. In brief, my views were: No silly 7-month puppy has homicidal tendencies. Those evil tendencies may or may not develop with age; though not once in hundreds of times will they do so, even then. Also, no pup nor grown dog tries deliberately to kill a swimmer by climbing on the swimmer's back. That is not canine nature. However, it is puppy nature (and adult dog nature sometimes), to romp with swimmers, by climbing playfully onto their shoulders.*[39]

Terhune went on to give Sessions advice on the ease by which someone is able to slip from a playful dog's grasp. He also gave Sessions a hint on what to look for on the body of the drowned boy and provided him with a drawing of the difference between cats' claws and the nails on dogs' paws.

All the swimmer need do would be to shake the animal loose or to roll sideways, ducking him; or to dive. A dog's claws are not like a cat's. Never does he dig them into anyone or anything. Canine claws are not built that way. They may scratch, inadvertently, but they cannot pierce. So, there could be no question of his sinking his talons into a victim, and of hanging on. It couldn't be done.[40]

As Sessions prepared for the trial, letters, telephone calls and telegrams continued to arrive for Benedict and Victor Fortune.

Justice of Peace
Homer B. Benedict
Brockport, N.Y.
Public is counting on your sanity to prevent hysterical destruction of playful Idaho. Am director S.P.C.A. Have over thirty dogs myself, mostly mongrels, any one of which will play in water or land. Couldn't owner keep dog away from swimming holes if neighbors are afraid.
Henrietta P. Carwithen[41]

Tilden Chapel of Brockport wrote to advance the theory that Idaho was trying to save the youth and suggested that he be given a chance in the water to prove he was capable of such a rescue.[42] An Upstate New York Humane Society sent a telegram.

Homer B. Benedict
Justice of the Peace
Brockport, N.Y.
Newspaper clipping re—dog Idaho would not indicate viciousness. (stop)
Urge you spare dog's life until most thorough investigation can be made. (stop)
Animal Humane Association, North Cohocton, N.Y., July 22, 1936 (stop)[43]

Another letter came from S.B. Curtis of the New York State Humane Society: "Idaho is not guilty of murder. The dog had no idea the harm he was doing. The whole case is ridiculous. A dog has not the brain of a man.

As a member of the state humane society, I protest. Let the dog go free. I shall watch the results."[44] Children sent money and messages. "The dog's legal defense team, on August 5th, announced the receipt of 10 cents from three Brockport children."[45] Another group of children, "Betty, Ruth, Billy Sidney and Jess Jarrett of Scottsville, who range in age from 3 to 11 years, sent pennies and wrote: 'We want to help Idaho.'"[46]

This next letter turns to sarcasm to make the same point made by Albert Payson Terhune, that no dog is capable of premeditated murder.

> *To Whom It May Concern:*
> *Your efforts to convict a dangerous criminal are noted and should be a warning to gangsters and criminals at large throughout the land. Probably "Idaho" is guilty of murder, first degree, because of premeditation—maybe he purchased candy or such to lure his victim to go in the Barge Canal July 4. Really, if such a vile criminal were to remain at large, it would not be safe for boys and small men to go swimming anymore.*
>
> *Truly, it is tragic about the poor lad, but how can any sane person instigate civil proceedings against a mere puppy? Did you ever happen to read at any time where a dog's efforts saved a child from drowning—or don't you read the papers?*
> *An admirer of dogs*
> *Albany, N.Y.*[47]

Many of the letters contained sarcasm, including one in which a boy asks Judge Benedict to put a mosquito on trial because it bit him. I doubt that the boy was aware that in medieval times formal trials were held for insects and other nonhuman subjects. The letter writer would be shocked to learn about trials for locusts, beetles and flies (more on that later).

Not all of the letters were sarcastic or in favor of Idaho. A distant neighbor of the Breezes, on West Avenue in Brockport, sent the judge the following letter:

> *Homer B. Benedict*
> *Brockport, N.Y.*
> *Dear Sir:*
> *I am writing in regard to the dog, Idaho, which is being tried for murder. Has everyone gone mad? How can anyone wish to give the life of an animal which is believed to have been the cause of a human being's death?*
>
> *I am an excellent swimmer, yet I am sure that a dog, even in fun, could so hamper my movements as to cause me to drown. I have a dog myself,*

of which I am very fond, but if he were accused of causing the death of
a person, whether in fun or otherwise, I should have him shot immediately.
We shoot dogs which kill sheep. Why let them kill people? Think of this
14-year-old boy who should have had his life before him, and his parents.
Also, the other children swimmers who may follow. What if it was done in
the spirit of fun? Is not that carrying fun too far?
Yours Sincerely,
Jennetta Polmateer
West Avenue
Brockport, N.Y.
July 22, 1936[48]

There were not only letters and telegrams. If Judge Benedict read the
newspapers, he would have seen that columnists were also trying to influence
public opinion. Henry Clune, a well-known columnist with the local *Democrat*
and Chronicle, denounced the sentimentality of people who put the life of a
dog above that of a young boy. In his "Seen and Heard" column, Clune
wrote that he felt that those who wanted Idaho's life spared were overlooking
the fact that a boy's life had been lost. He went on to say that he wished
the same amount of effort directed toward saving a dog's life would be put
toward saving the lives of children.[49]

None other than the famous dancer Irene Castle, of the husband-and-
wife team of ballroom dancers who appeared on Broadway and in silent
films in the early part of the twentieth century, entered the fray, declaring:
"It is absurd to try something that can't defend itself. There certainly was
no premeditation on the dog's part. I'm sure the death of the boy was an
accident." Irene Castle even said that she would be delighted to take Idaho
into her Orphans of the Storm dog shelter near Chicago.[50]

The same division evident in the Village of Brockport is shown in the
letters received by Justice Benedict. The other side of the controversy is
expressed in the next letter.

Mr. Homer B. Benedict
Attorney-at-Law
Brockport, N.Y.
Dear Mr. Benedict:
At the present time the front page of the second section of the Democrat
and Chronicle is filled with the most ridiculous and sensational bit of
journalism that anyone in his most imaginative mood could ever concede.

To think that this cultured age of civilization could wish the life of this mongrel pup to be spared in face of the fact that he was guilty of the death of a human being, is beyond comprehension. Although not fully aware of the technicalities of the case, I have assumed that "Idaho" is the dog which so "playfully" caused the death of Maxwell Breeze in the Barge Canal on July 4.

Has anyone ever tried to assume the position of the grief-stricken parents? Apparently not. An invalid mother, whose very heart and soul centered around the life of her son, now suddenly finds him gone. Doesn't anyone ever think of her and the sorrowing father? Has anyone given any publicity to Paul Hamlin who valiantly sought to save his playmate from the paws of death? No.

On the other hand, a young man is in danger of losing his pet, a mongrel dog. It is easily seen how one may become attached to a dog, but when it results in placing a dog on an equal basis with human beings, it is so ridiculous that it becomes pathetic.

Assuming that the dog is only "playful" should it not be removed from the community where it has caused one death and is likely to cause more?

Will the people of Brockport allow the life of a mongrel dog to outweigh the life of an intelligent, gifted young man of fourteen? Only time will tell and may the mercy of God rest upon the final judgment.

Very respectfully yours,
Milo R Freson, Jr.[51]

Judge Benedict was also the recipient of a threatening letter. Signed "Black Legion" and bearing a skull and crossbones, it contained a warning to Homer B. Benedict that there would be "trouble" if he failed "to get that dog."[52]

But the most unusual letters received were from dogs. One came from a dog named "Kentucky Boy" (more on Kentucky Boy later) and another from the New York Humane Society mascot, "Paddy." "As a dog who has saved many lives, both human and animal, I plead for fair play for Idaho."[53]

Victor Fortune was also the recipient of letters of support. One letter, from a doctor, expressed great concern for Idaho and proceeded for two typewritten pages to outline the history of dogs in antiquity, specific breeds of dogs and their characteristics and advice on defending Idaho in court. It began as follows:

Charles A. Smith, M.D.
New Rochelle, NY
July 31, 1936
Dear Victor,
I have been deeply concerned about your dog, Idaho, for some time and trust that you have a lawyer to argue the defense for him.[54]

The time between the hearing and trial proved to be difficult for the Fortune family. Not only was there the worry of the trial and Idaho's fate, but there was also anxiety over the fundraising and the division in the community. They were also subjected to some animosity. Victor said that his mother took it the hardest.

Folks were so mixed in their feelings. People wanted Idaho killed, called my family names while others were starting to talk about a fund to defend the dog. We didn't have any money to defend Idaho. Mom stood tall defending the dog despite the fact that she was only 5 foot two. She cried for Max's Mother but also for Idaho.[55]

To add to the stress, the story was front and center in local newspapers and radio programs. The *Brockport Republic and Brockport Democrat* ran a poll to see just how divided the community was.

Sentiment being so divided we are printing on this page a form for you to fill out. The results of this straw vote will be given to Judge Homer B. Benedict next Monday so if you are interested fill out the form and mail or bring it to this office not later than Saturday. Votes received in the mail Monday morning will be accepted.
It is not necessary for you to sign your name but you may if you want.

Idaho Straw Vote
Life Should Be Spared ____
Life Should Be Taken ____
He Is Dangerous ____
He Is Just Playful ____
Remarks ____[56]

Ada Fortune (Victor's mother) with flowers. *Photograph in the collection of Laurie Verbrdge.*

The poll only stirred up more controversy. On Monday, August 3, the *Democrat and Chronicle* published the following item in response to the poll from defense attorney Harry A. Sessions:

> *Sessions last night registered a protest against the poll. "I don't think it is proper practice," he said, "to express public opinion on a case to be decided by a judge. The Bar Association is traditionally against it. If this were a civil case in Supreme Court it would constitute grounds for the setting aside of a verdict."*[57]

Whether Judge Benedict ever saw the results of the poll is not known, but the *Brockport Republic and Democrat* reported that 196 readers favored putting Idaho down, while 187 preferred that he be set free. The paper also reported that votes received after the Monday deadline were not counted but would have been enough to call the poll a draw. The newspaper also reported that the poll caused "considerable interest not only in Brockport but throughout the United States."[58]

As the trial date approached, reporters, photographers and camera crews began to descend on the Village of Brockport. Judge Benedict moved the trial to the Town Hall in order to accommodate the 300 or more spectators and media. The night before the trial, citizens petitioned Judge Benedict to change the location of the trial to the Strand Theater on the grounds that the Town Hall was too small and would accommodate only 250 people. Benedict, who had already moved the hearing once—from his office to the Town Hall—demurred. The Brockport Hook and Ladder Company, which shared the Town Hall with the village offices, offered to move equipment outside so that the media had room to operate and lights could be set up for Paramount News and its "The Eyes and Ears of the World." The stage was already set for an event far bigger than any local amateur theater production. The actors, sets, lights and cameras were in place. The big question was, What would happen when the curtain went up?

4

WHAT IS GOING ON HERE?

Anyone who has read this far could well be wondering how such a seemingly local incident could have exploded into a nationwide spectacle. "All of the trappings of a Bruno Hauptmann trial," announced one media critic.[59] Was the Brockport "murder dog" trial actually being compared to the famous Lindbergh baby kidnapping trial—a trial described as "the trial of the century,"[60] "a media circus" and journalist H.L. Mencken's obvious exaggeration, "the greatest story since the Resurrection?"[61]

The Lindbergh kidnapping and subsequent trial of Bruno Hauptmann was fresh in the minds of the public in 1936. The kidnapping and murder of Charles and Anne Morrow Lindbergh's son took place in 1932, and the investigation leading to the arrest of Bruno Hauptmann was news from 1932 until 1934. The trial took place in 1935, and Hauptmann was executed in Trenton, New Jersey, only three months before the Brockport trial. The Bruno Hauptmann trial was a media circus, with seven hundred reporters, cameramen and cinematographers descending on Flemington, New Jersey. There were also five thousand spectators—nearly double the population of the town. The prosecutors called witnesses to testify as to the cloth and stitching in the child's sleeping garments, fingerprints, handwriting, wood structure of the ladder used to reach the second-floor nursery window, and an endless array of other witnesses.

The Brockport trial did have many reporters, cameramen and cinematographers, and, like the Flemington, New Jersey courthouse, the Brockport Town Hall overflowed with spectators. However, it seems a gross exaggeration to compare it to the Bruno Hauptmann trial. Was there another factor that attracted so much attention? An editorial in a Bangor, Maine newspaper suggested an answer to this question.

> *Have trials of human beings become so dull or have habitual trialgoers become so blasé that it is necessary to add an animal act? Are we to have trials of cats for mayhem, of parrots for libel and slander, of mules for felonious assault? Are learned judges to cite such cases as the State vs. one Pekinese and two wire-haired terriers, or John Smith vs. Neighbor Brown's pet cat? Perhaps some of those who gave expression to their mawkishness in cheers might pause to reflect on the trials of animals in the Middle Ages and on pitying the things we customarily say about such benighted times.*[62]

Was all of this attention on Brockport because an animal was on trial? The *Bangor Daily News* editorial raises a good point about reflecting on animal trials in the Middle Ages. How unusual was it for an animal to be on trial for its life? What can we learn about the Brockport "murder dog" case from animal trials of the Middle Ages? "'Once upon a time,'—and we might well begin in that manner because the story is as fantastic as a fairy tale—animals were held to be as liable as men for their criminal acts and torts."[63]

Idaho's case was not the first involving a dog in the history of criminal law. It is not even unique in trials involving animals. E.P. Evans's famous book *The Criminal Prosecution and Capital Punishment of Animals* gives 191 examples of animals—bulls, pigs, goats, rats, roosters, dogs and cats—put on trial for their lives for various misdeeds.

A comment in one letter sent to Judge Benedict asking that a mosquito be put on trial for biting the letter writer is exactly what happened during the Middle Ages, when all sorts of insects (locusts, grasshoppers, weevils, caterpillars, beetles and flies) were put on trial. If there was any suspicion that mosquitos were spreading a disease among the population, they would certainly have joined the long list of insects put on trial.

Historians believe that Evans's list of 191 animal trials is only a fraction of such trials that took place in the Middle Ages. His list is limited by the fact that, during the Middle Ages, and even later, court records were often poorly kept, lost or completely destroyed. Because of this, we are left with an incomplete history of these trials, and the existing records of these prosecutions almost certainly represent only a few of the cases that actually took place. There is no better example of this than the Brockport trial, in which information in the summons is written by hand in the margins of the document and over headings, and after only eighty years, no court records exist and most of the information available is the result of contemporary news reports on the trial.

The works of contemporary writers (as is the case with the 1936 Brockport trial) supplement court and other historical records. The fact that contemporary writers used these cases in their works suggests that post-medieval Europeans were familiar with these animal trials.[64] Shakespeare, in act 4, scene 1 of *The Merchant of Venice* (1600), refers to a murder trial of a wolf that took place in the medieval era: "Thy currish spirit. Governed a wolf who hanged for human slaughter."[65] Of course, animal trials continued during the time of Shakespeare and beyond. Evans was still reporting a wolf trial in 1891.[66]

In the latter half of the seventeenth century, the French playwright Jean Racine parodied a medieval animal trial of which his audience was evidently familiar. Again, in Evans's list of 191 animal trials, 45 occurred from 1650 to 1906, so Racine's audience was aware of the medieval trials, but they also must have been aware that animals were still being brought to trial in the seventeenth century.[67]

In Racine's *Les Plaideurs* (*The Litigants*, 1668), the farce-like nature of the play is depicted in its climactic final trial of the judge's dog Citron, who is accused of having stolen a capon in the kitchen. While Citron is making his appearance before the court, his defense, to try to persuade the judge to be lenient, presents Citron's puppies, which would become orphans if Citron were sentenced to death. The puppies, being puppies, produce a puddle on the courtroom floor, and the lawyer presents the resulting puddle as caused by teardrops.[68] "This strikes us as simply farcical and not very funny; but to Racine's audience it was a mirror reflecting a characteristic feature of the time and ridiculing grave judicial abuse."[69]

Examples in later literature refer to the prosecution of animals. In the classic novel *The Hunchback of Notre Dame* (1833), Victor Hugo details the fifteenth-century trial of Esmeralda's goat. ("Nothing was more common in those times than to bring a charge of witchcraft against animals.")[70]

Both Racine's and Shakespeare's references suggest that the trials and executions of animals were common in Europe in the Middle Ages and later—or at least that they occurred frequently enough that Shakespeare, Racine and other writers could use them in their plays with the confidence that their audiences would recognize them. The fact that the records of many of these trials are incomplete or lost is no surprise. We need only look back as far as 1936 to find that trial transcripts can be lost, discarded or destroyed and that we need modern journalists and playwrights to fill in the details of the trial for us.

Most of these animal trials occurred in medieval Europe during much different times. Many of the trials have to do with witchcraft, superstition and religious doctrine, and many place animals before the judicial bench that we might laugh at. A case in point—although at first it might seem as far removed as the years between 1457 and 1936—is the trial in France of a pig that, along with her six piglets, killed a child. All seven pigs were caught in the act, imprisoned and eventually brought to trial. Esther Cohen, the author of *Law, Folklore, and Animal Lore*, notes that from the very beginning of the legal proceedings, it was clear that the owner of the pig—though formally the defendant—was accused only of negligence and faced no actual punishment for the death of five-year-old Jehan Martin. The pig, on the other hand, faced the death sentence.[71]

Such a case might seem bizarre to modern observers, but animals that allegedly broke the law were routinely subjected to the same legal proceedings as humans. In a court of law, they were treated as persons. These trials,

Pig on trial, 1457. *Reproduced by the author.*

which always adhered to the strictest legal procedures, reveal a medieval belief that some animals possessed moral responsibility.[72]

Animals tried in medieval courts were held responsible for their misdeeds, were provided the same procedures and protections as humans, were given legal representation and were punished—all in a manner that mirrored the treatment of human defendants. Idaho, as were his medieval forebears, was provided with procedures and protections of a normal trial and received legal counsel. He also could be punished by death or confinement.

The Brockport trial was sensationalized by the media as a case about a dog accused of murdering young Maxwell Breeze. Actually, the trial was about another incident involving a different swimmer who survived his encounter with a dog in the canal. The owner of the dog, Victor Fortune, was charged with harboring a vicious dog and faced a minor fine and court costs. His dog, Idaho, was on trial for his life, just as in the case of the pig in 1457.

Having a pig on trial seems very strange today but, during medieval times, pigs were a very common sight in towns and villages and roamed quite freely. In many ways, dogs occupy a place in our lives similar to that occupied by pigs in medieval villages. Nowadays, pigs are confined out of sight, but dogs live with us and are with us all the time, as pigs used to be. Dogs and humans have a bond based on the sharing of day-to-day lives. Because of their number and close association, there are times when dogs can and do harm humans. The punishment of animals, such as a pig, had to be weighed against the fact that the pig was a crucial economic asset for a family in a peasant economy, the loss of which could be disastrous. Today, it is dogs that are animals of great value to us—a value that is primarily emotional but must be taken into account when a final sentence is passed down from the bench.

The 1457 trial had other similarities to Idaho's trial. Fifteenth-century French pigs that committed felonies went to court. The 1457 trial was a real trial with a judge, two prosecutors, eight witnesses and a defense attorney for the accused swine. Witness testimony proved beyond a reasonable doubt that the sow killed a child. Similarly, the Brockport trial had a judge, a prosecutor (Costigan) and twenty-seven witnesses and a defense attorney for the accused dog. Another common item, pointed out by Albert Terhune, was the false presumption that an animal had the capacity to commit murder— "a mentality according to which some animals possessed moral agency."[73]

In 1771, Edward Long published *The Trial of farmer Carter's dog Porter, for Murder*, a satire on British society, judicial abuses, game laws and animal trials. "Porter," the defendant, was treated as a human and given demands by the magistrates like, "Hold up your right paw." When Porter did not respond, there was argument back and forth over why the dog did not do as he was ordered. Finally, the defense counsel lifted the dog's right paw. Not to be discouraged, the magistrate then asked Porter, "How do you plead?" When Porter refused to respond, there ensued a long discussion of whether silence meant guilt or lack of guilt. The defense attorney then demanded a trial by a jury of his peers, a precursor of a trial 150 years later in the United States, and that was followed by a long discussion of which breeds of dogs represented the peer of a sheepdog. In a situation similar to the trial of the pig and her piglets and the parody by Racine of the dog and her puppies, Porter did not produce a puddle on the floor but wet the leg of the prosecutor. One part of the trial mirrored medieval animal trials when, in order to give animals the same justice as humans, the court debated torturing the dog to obtain a confession. In this satire on British game laws, Porter was accused of murdering a hare on a nobleman's estate. When the defense asked the prosecution to produce the body of the murder victim, they were informed that the rabbit had been eaten for dinner. By the end of the trial, farmer Carter had been forcibly removed from the court and Porter was found guilty and hanged.[74]

Animal trials exist, according to one explanation given by legal scholars and historians, "in a society of people who believe deeply in a divinely determined order of being, with humans at the top. Any disruption of God's hierarchy had to be visibly restored with a formal event."[75] This thinking may have come into play in the Brockport trial with a comment by Maxwell Breeze's mother: "Well, it comes down to whether you value the life of a dog above the life of a boy."[76] Anna Breeze expected that the formal event (Idaho's trial) would restore the proper order of things.

McWilliams, in his article "Beastly Justice," suggests a biblical reason for the harsh sentences imposed on offending animals.

In other cases where an animal has seriously injured or killed a person, it seems that the motive behind killing the offending animal is to restore the hierarchical order that the animal, by its actions, has upset. Like the goring ox or infanticidal pig, today's animal offenders pose a real threat to the hierarchical order set out in the Book of Genesis, which places human beings above all other forms of life. It is not too far a stretch to suggest that when animals are killed for their offenses, the executions are motivated, either in whole or in part, because the transgressing animals do not conform to their place in the scheme of things. Animals are not supposed to injure or kill human beings....When animals cause harm—especially physical injury—to people, they violate the strict hierarchy and "natural" order of things. Thus, for perhaps one of the same reasons the medieval Europeans punished animals who failed to observe this separation of the species, so we, too, restore order by punishing transgressing animals.[77]

Anna Breeze, being a religious woman, obviously believed what is written in Genesis 1:28, that man shall have "dominion over the fish in the sea; the fowl in the air; and over every living thing that moves upon the earth."[78]

The last animal prosecution listed in Evans's book, in 1906, is the trial of a dog. In Delémont, Switzerland, a man named Mager was robbed and killed by a father-son team with the cooperation of their dog. All three suspects—the two men as well as the dog—were tried for the crime. The court sentenced the two men to life in prison. The dog, however, "as the chief culprit, without whose complicity the crime could not have been committed," was given a death sentence.[79] It has been pointed out that in most instances of a human owner and a dog on trial, the dog is on trial for its life, while the human, as in the Brockport trial, faces only court costs and a small fine.

The historic trend is of dog trials becoming more frequent and pig trials less frequent as we move toward the twentieth century. Between 1266 and 1510, Evans lists twenty-two trials in which pigs were the defendants. The first listing of a trial involving a dog does not appear until 1525. From the beginning of the seventeenth century to the twentieth century, only two pigs are put on trial. In contrast, Evans lists six dogs tried for various misdeeds.[80] Animal jurisprudence had definitely gone to the dogs.

Aside from the fact that animal trials, in modern times, are unusual, what else was driving the Brockport trial into such a frenzy? Was it the media? Was it an overzealous or overcautious judge? Was it because the hearings went beyond hearings and into a full-blown trial? Was it because Idaho became the defendant? Was it because of an overzealous lawyer who subpoenaed over thirty witnesses? Was it a slow news time? Was it the Great Depression? Was there something else about the 1930s that evoked such a universal response?

The media coverage did more than give the trial notoriety. The newspapers constantly referred to the trial as a murder trial. There was barely a pause before one sensational headline after another appeared in newspapers all across the country: "Dog Accused of Murder on Trial for Life Today"; Brockport Tragedy Led to Dog's Trial for Murder"; "Dog on Trial Charged with Murder of Boy"; "Mongrel on Trial for Life in Death of Child"; "Alibi Dog May Deliver Mongrel from Execution on Murder Charge"; "Master

Hides Dog Facing Murder Trial." The media seemed to jump on any new development—or even a perceived development—in the case.

The newspapers used the term *murder dog*. The trial itself seldom mentioned the word *murder*. The issue was whether Idaho was vicious or dangerous and should be destroyed. Witnesses were asked if the dog was dangerous, but the prosecutor and the defendant's lawyer avoided asking if the dog was a murderer. Was this case so sensational because, as one journalist put it, "It was the most spectacular case involving a dog in the history of criminal law?"[81]

Was the trial necessary? The New York State vicious animal statute only asks a judge to decide if an animal is vicious based on an examination of the evidence and the report of a state-certified veterinarian. Judge Benedict could have made his decision after the hearing and a report from the vet. That would have done away with the two-week hiatus when the whole thing exploded into a national sensation. The required hearing had already been held; all the judge had to do was wait for the veterinarian's report and make his ruling. Maybe, after thirty-four years on the bench, Homer Benedict was wiser than anyone suspected. Given the emotion surrounding this case, he decided to let the public express its opinions and, as in the medieval animal trials, he would provide the public with a display of formal judicial procedure.

> *Although the old trials were formally framed as the provision of procedural fairness to the animal defendants, at least part of the underlying motivation may have been a reluctance to deprive human members of the community of something of great value to them without following the rudimentary requirements of natural justice—an opportunity to be heard, to put forward evidence and arguments to try to influence the decision. As may be the case in at least some modern "dog trials," the legal proceedings have probably only created additional stress.*[82]

The Brockport trial did give the residents plenty of opportunity to express their opinions—in letters, telegrams, newspaper polls, boos, hisses and applause. But it also created additional stress on almost everyone except Idaho, who was oblivious to everything except being separated from his owner. It certainly added stress to the Fortune family, which was affected by the events leading up to the trial, the trial itself and the events after the trial. Even though the trial was not about the death of Maxwell Breeze, it might as well have been. Anna and William Breeze suffered the added stress of losing their only son, listening to descriptions of how he died and of the appearance of his body and hearing the judge's final decision, to which William Breeze muttered, "It doesn't suit me."

The *New York Times* reported on the traditional aspects of the trial, the environment surrounding the trial and that the facts in the case were simple. "Though the framework of a modern murder trial was there, with its conscious theatrics, in the hard, hot glare of Klieg lights, the fundamental facts remained peculiarly simple and dramatic."[83]

Could it be that in most trials involving dogs killing people, the owner, not the dog, is charged? Victor Fortune was charged with harboring a dangerous animal, but Idaho became the focus, even though the charges were brought by Daniel Houghton for two attacks on his person. In the end, if Victor was found to be harboring a vicious or dangerous dog, the dog could be euthanized. Is it possible that people had more sympathy for the dog than for the owner? Suddenly, in the press, Victor Fortune, the owner of Idaho, was not the subject of this trial—Idaho was. Victor served as defender and a witness as to Idaho's disposition. The trial was held to determine if Idaho was a vicious or dangerous dog. The *Democrat and Chronicle* called it "the only 'murder' trial on record of a dog,"[84] a misstatement if there ever was one.

Was the trial blown out of proportion because Harry A. Sessions went overboard with his defense by subpoenaing over thirty witnesses? Sessions even went to the trouble of searching out a local dog that resembled Idaho in order to question the witness identifications. The "alibi dog" made national headlines.[85] Calling in national experts for a small-town hearing on a vicious dog case would seem to be excessive, as would registering objections threatening to have the verdict overturned if the newspaper poll was released to Judge Benedict. Albert Payson Terhune said, "Sessions went to work on the case with all of the zeal and skill he might have employed if his client had had two legs instead of four."[86] The *New York Times* wrote, "All the fanfare of an important criminal case attended the preparations."[87] The *Times* went on to say, "Before the sentence was pronounced there had been written into the records of Sweden Township an amazing profusion of testimony, cross-examination and re-direct examination, oratory and irrelevance."[88]

This is exactly what writers three hundred years earlier had said. Compare this "amazing profusion of testimony, cross-examination and re-direct examination, oratory and irrelevance" with act 1, scene 7 from the Racine farce mentioned earlier:

> *Another incident: while we are working at the trial. My opponent lets his chickens peck on my farm. I requested that a report be made to the*

court on the amount of hay a chicken can eat in one day. After all this is joined to the proceedings, the appointment of the trial date is made for the fifth or the sixth of April fifty-six. I write again from scratch. I furnish Plaints, requests, enquiries, discovery orders, experts' opinions and interim judgments, new causes and facts, lease contracts and records, royal letters, even a plea of forgery. Fourteen appointments, thirty services, six claims, ten dozen productions, twenty injunctions. At last the sentence. I lose the case at my expense, estimated at roughly five to six thousand francs. Is this right? Is this how justice should be done? After fifteen or twenty years! I have a last resort: I can still lodge an appeal for review. My case is not yet lost.[89]

Whether or not the Brockport trial required this profusion of testimony, Sessions obviously did his homework. As the trial proceeded, it became obvious that Sessions was aware of previous dog trials and the tactics used to defend the animals. In his final summation, Sessions used an emotional appeal and, in one part, the exact words contained in the summations of a previous dog trial.

How much did Mary Foubister influence the trial, its publicity and its outcome? She came to see Victor Fortune shortly before the hearing and within days of receiving the "notice" to appear before Justice Benedict. Mary was the one who suggested that Victor place Idaho in the care of the Rochester Dog Protective Association. She may have been the one who deliberately "hid" Idaho by not bringing him to the hearing. She interjected herself into the proceedings of the July 21 hearing, even though she was not on the witness list contained in the court docket. "Dr. William H. Mahoney and Mary Foubister were sworn and testified *at the request of Mary Foubister,* Executive Secretary of the Rochester Dog Protective Society."[90]

Mary also was the one who obtained the delay from July 21 to August 5. She was the one who suggested obtaining a lawyer and suggested Harry Sessions. Mary was also at the forefront of the fundraising activities. She had Idaho photographed with a rabbit to demonstrate how gentle he was and released the photo to the local paper before the trial began to try to stir up public opinion. Her testimony at the hearing also influenced the court to use the Rochester Dog Protective Association's own veterinarian to observe Idaho's behavior. Although Harry Sessions is often given most of the credit, it was Mary Foubister who ran the show.

What happened to fuel all of this frenzy was probably not a single factor, but a combination of factors. The frenzy kept building, to the point that the story went far beyond its small-town origins. Of course, the case was important to the people directly affected by the outcome of the trial—the Breezes and the Fortunes—and, most of all, Idaho. To almost everyone else, especially the media, it was entertainment.

The day before the trial, it was certainly not entertaining for the Fortune family. Even listening to the radio proved to be difficult. Newspapers and newsreels were not the only media covering the case. Victor describes the state of anxiety the family was in.

August 4 was my Mother's birthday. I came home to help celebrate and she was a mess. "I am so afraid for tomorrow, Victor! Today, I turned on the radio and it was all about the poll and people wanting Idaho to be executed. I had to turn it off. I couldn't stand it."

"Pop"—my Dad—and Norm were reviewing their testimony during the day with Harry. They were really nervous. My brother Jack was young enough that he felt that no one would execute Idaho because he was just a playful puppy! Also, he knew for sure that Idaho was on property all day 4th of July. "It had to be the other dog! Idaho would never hurt anyone! I intend to tell them that tomorrow when I testify!"

I reassured all of them and said, "be sure you answer the questions that Mr. Sessions asks you. No more, no less. Less is often better." I reassured my Mother that Harry Sessions and Mary had everything under control and that they would save Idaho. Tomorrow we would know for sure. I went to bed. I wished Idaho was home but knew that he was safer with Mary. I barely slept. Over and over in my mind I went over my testimony. I started to think, what if everything goes south and Idaho is executed? I tried to get that thought out of my mind but I couldn't.[91]

5

THE MURDER DOG TRIAL

Part 1

On the day of the trial, "The Eyes and Ears of the World" Paramount crew was busy filming along the Erie Canal, which was located directly across from the Town Hall, and on the steps of the Town Hall. The crew also filmed Idaho behind bars; the Erie Canal; Mary Foubister, secretary of the Rochester Dog Protective Association; Maxwell Breeze's friends, lying on the grass by the canal; William and Anna Breeze on the front steps of their home on East Avenue; and Justice of the Peace Homer B. Benedict.

Maxie's friends were discussing Idaho's role in the drowning.

> *1ˢᵗ boy: Do you think the dog Idaho is responsible for Maxie's death?*
> *2ⁿᵈ boy: He was responsible for the drowning, but every dog likes to play like that and I don't think that he should die. He was just playing with Max out there in the water.*[92]

On the newsreel, Anna and William Breeze sat side by side on the steps of their home on East Avenue. Anna spoke first.

> *Anna Breeze: Well, it comes down to whether you value the life of a dog above the life of a boy.*
> *William Breeze: All my life I've been a lover of dogs, but if this dog is found guilty in the death of my child, I demand that he be executed.*[93]

DOG ON TRIAL CHARGED WITH MURDER OF BOY

Paramount News

Left: Paramount News logo, 1936. *Grinberg Paramount Pathe Inc., used with permission.*

Below: Maxwell Breeze's friends. *Grinberg Paramount Pathe Inc., used with permission.*

Then Victor Fortune spoke. "I've owned this dog for seven months and he wouldn't purposely drown a boy."[94]

Paramount News was successful in enticing Judge Benedict to sit down before the camera and say: "I shall endeavor to decide whether or not Idaho is a dangerous dog or not. If so found, he will be shot or confined. If not dangerous, he will be free."[95]

Acting as a spokesman for the Rochester Dog Protective Association, Mary Foubister appeared briefly on camera.

Above: Justice Homer B. Benedict. *Grinberg Paramount Pathe Inc., used with permission.*

Opposite, top: William and Anna Breeze. *Grinberg Paramount Pathe Inc., used with permission.*

Opposite, bottom: Victor Fortune. *Grinberg Paramount Pathe Inc., used with permission.*

> *Mary Foubister: As chairman of the Idaho Defense Fund, I am convinced that Idaho is not a killer. I will put forth every effort to save his life.*[96]

After the Paramount newsreel crew finished interviewing those involved in the trial, Victor, appearing off camera, recalled what he did the morning of the trial.

> *The next day I got there early and met with Harry one more time for a few minutes. Mary joined us. While the case could go either way, they were well prepared to defend Idaho's life.*
>
> *When we returned to the area of the Brockport Village Hall where they usually kept the fire trucks, it was packed with people. I was glad the weather was cooler because that building was warm as it was. The cameras were flashing on us and I was amazed at how many photographers*

Above: Mary Foubister and Idaho. *Grinberg Paramount Pathe Inc., used with permission.*

Opposite, top: Brockport Town Hall, August 5, 1936. *Grinberg Paramount Pathe Inc., used with permission.*

Opposite, bottom: Crowded courtroom. *Grinberg Paramount Pathe Inc., used with permission.*

there were. The people of the community were there. I knew who was on Idaho's side and who was not.[97]

Joseph R. Ware was Idaho's bodyguard who was placed on duty when Idaho's life was threatened to avoid him being killed at the shelter or for fear that he might be stolen. Joe brought Idaho to court that day. Joe had once served as a bodyguard to President Taft. He took care of Idaho's safety twenty-four hours a day.

When Idaho saw me, he was so excited. I had to calm him down. Everyone was petting him as he entered the Village Hall. I stood behind the judge and Mr. Breeze sat in a chair across from us. It was hard to look at him because I knew how sad he was, but I believed with all my heart that Idaho was innocent of murder.[98]

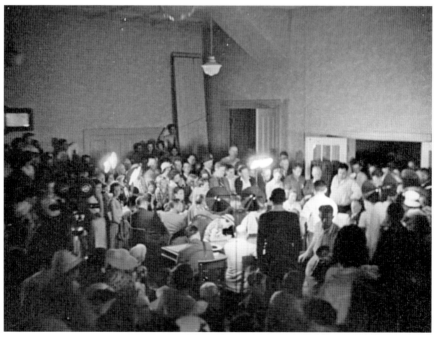

Idaho being led by Deputy Oren Tuttle into Town Hall. *Grinberg Paramount Pathe Inc., used with permission.*

As the time for the trial approached, spectators, reporters, photographers and the newsreel crew and their added lights filled every available space in the courtroom, corridors and stairs. More space was added by Brockport Hook and Ladder, which moved equipment in order to make room for the press. People in the courtroom filled every chair, sat on windowsills and radiators and on any available surface. Others stood throughout the five-hour trial. It was estimated that five hundred spectators attended the Brockport "murder dog" trial. A reporter described the scene in the town hall. "Shortly before 10 a.m., the high-ceilinged, gray room was filled with farmers, blinking every time a flashlight went off, matrons with worried expressions, gawky schoolgirls, scores of squirmy boys, many with lollypops, and the greatest array of newsreel and photographic apparatus ever assembled in Brockport."[99]

The film crew moved inside, and the camera panned an overcrowded courtroom. Just before 10:00 a.m., Deputy Sheriff Oren J. Tuttle, filmed by the movie crew, led Idaho, on a chain leash, up the sidewalk, lined on both sides with spectators eager to see the dog.

"We'll call the case now," said Justice Benedict.

Technically, this was not a murder trial. Idaho was to be tried under a farm and market law providing for the destruction of vicious animals. Thus, unlike a criminal trial, in which the prosecution presents its case first, followed by the defense, it was up to the defense to prove that the animal was not vicious and should not be destroyed.

Judge Benedict quickly, and in a voice barely audible, read the New York State statutes that applied to the case.

> *A dog shall not be declared dangerous if the court determines the conduct of the dog (a) was justified because the threat, injury or damage was sustained by a person who at the time was committing a crime or offense upon the owner or custodian of the dog or upon the property of the owner or custodian of the dog; (b) was justified because the injured, threatened or killed person was tormenting, abusing, assaulting or physically threatening the dog or its offspring, or has in the past tormented, abused, assaulted or physically threatened the dog or its offspring; (c) was justified because the dog was responding to pain or injury, or was protecting itself, owner.*[100]

At the trial, police officer James Costigan served as prosecuting attorney (Judge Benedict was also free to question witnesses), and Harry Sessions was the defense attorney. Idaho remained in the courtroom for the entire trial—occasionally alert, sometimes sleeping and a few times even barking.

Justice Benedict then told Harry Sessions to begin. Sessions began by calling George Fortune, fifty, father of Idaho's owner. George told the court that Idaho was home the entire day on July 4. He said he saw Max Breeze and the other boys leave the ball diamond near his home. "Idaho was on the porch. I noticed particularly because he was playing with a large stick."

> *Q. Was the dog wet at any time on the day of the drowning?*
> *A. No.*[101]

Costigan cross-examined the witness sharply by finding some holes in the timeline.

Jack Fortune, Victor Fortune's ten-year-old brother, was called next. He insisted that Idaho was not wet at any time on July 4.

Next to take the stand was Frank Morass, a neighbor of the Fortunes.

> *Q. How would you describe Idaho's disposition?*
> *A. Very playful.*

Left: Jack Fortune (Victor Fortune's brother). *Photograph in author's collection.*

Below: Frank Morass, neighbor and witness for the defense. *Grinberg Paramount Pathe Inc., used with permission.*

Q. Did you ever know Idaho to attack anyone?
A. No! replied Morass explosively.

His answer was followed by a bark from Idaho so similar in sound to that of the witness that it evoked laughter in the courtroom.

"You have him well trained," Judge Benedict said to Sessions.[102]

Next, Victor Fortune, owner of the dog, took the stand. Fortune told the court that Idaho was one of a litter of puppies he took care of while working at a Civilian Conservation Corps camp at Salmon, Idaho. When Victor came east on a troop train, Idaho came with him.[103] Sessions called Clem Snover, eighteen, a neighbor of the Fortunes, to the stand. Snover said that when he heard there was an accident at the canal, he grabbed his bathing suit off the line in his backyard and ran to the canal.

Q. What were they doing when you arrived?
A. They were dragging for Max's body.
Q. Did you see a dog there?
A. Yes.
Q. Was the dog in or out of the water?
A. Out of the water.
Q. Was he wet?
A. Yes.
Q. Do you know the dog Idaho?
A. Yes.
Q. Tell the judge if the dog you saw was Idaho or not.
A. The dog I saw was not Idaho.
Q. Was there another dog there?
A. Yes. The dog I saw looked vicious.[104]

As the trial continued and, possibly acting on the information from the dog expert, Albert Payson Terhune, Sessions called witness William Brady, a morgue attendant.

Q. Were there any scratches on Maxwell's body when you examined it?
A. No.[105]

Walter Welsh, who helped pull Max Breeze out of the Erie Canal, took the stand and testified to much the same thing as had Brady. Welsh was followed by Peter Gallo, Norman Fortune (one of Victor Fortune's younger brothers) and Anthony Barber.[106]

Victor Fortune. *Grinberg Paramount Pathe Inc., used with permission.*

Victor Fortune's recollection of the trial was that of a never-ending change of emotions, from calm to agitation, from fear to excitement and from sadness to hopefulness.

> *During the trial Idaho was pretty docile and quiet until my Dad testified. I remember feeling very nervous and thinking I should calm him. Another time he barked like he was answering questions and Judge Benedict made a joke out of it. The trial lasted about five hours. I thought it would never end. Sometimes I was excited and felt the testimony was in our favor. When the boys testified, I felt sad and dismayed. No matter what, I knew that Idaho was not guilty of murdering Max.*[107]

As the trial continued, the *New York Times* reported that "500 men, women and children muttered, gaped and fidgeted in the weathered Village Hall during an unparalleled 'legal' proceeding."[108] After two and a half hours, Justice Benedict called for a half-hour recess.

6

FIVE DOG TRIAL

Dog Number 1

The Brockport "murder dog" trial involved not one dog, but five dogs. Idaho was, of course, the center of international attention. His owner, Victor Fortune, describes how he came into possession of the dog.

I tried to work for nearly a year when I re-enlisted in the CCC's April 24th for another year long stint. I was able to hook up with my former company 1254. Company 1254 had completed the jobs that were set forth in the Enfield Park and forest fires were rampant along the Salmon River in Idaho. Camp 1254 New York was hosted by Camp F-176 Salmon Idaho. I was there from July until January. Upon arrival I was greeted at Camp F-176 by a black German shepherd named Captain and his girlfriend Queenie. She was a bit of an Airedale/lab mix with German shepherd ears. It was so good to be with dogs and Queenie took an instant liking to me. We had always had dogs at home and I missed them. Queenie was rather plump, and I suspected she was pregnant. We would come home at night after a long day of hot fires and trucking dirt for the roads to the fire and Queenie would look for me. She actually belonged to Camp F176 and had come as a stray. Our Sergeant owned Captain and he said when he left the assignment, he would take both dogs with him.

Queenie gave birth September 20, 1935 to 7 pups. I was the first one to find her because she had her pups under my bed. We made a box for her

Above: CCC camp, Salmon River, Idaho. *Photograph in author's collection.*

Left: Idaho as a puppy. *Photograph in author's collection.*

with the babies near Captain. What fun we had with those puppies. When Idaho opened his eyes, he was the biggest and I put a piece of string around his neck and said I would take him. I was lucky to get one as the pups were in big demand!

Once Idaho was weaned, I began taking him with me in my CCC truck. He trained really easy and was very smart. He'd sit up on that seat and made lots of friends on our travels. He would come with me wherever I went and he was a great companion. In mid-November, I introduced him to swimming. Idaho loved the water, running along the beach and in and out! I went in to my knees as the water in the Salmon River was freezing but he didn't seem to mind it!

Idaho started sleeping at the foot of my bed. Often, I could not move my feet because he was so close to me. He had a hard time getting up there at first but it wasn't long before he could make the big leap. He was pretty funny making sure he got up there.

On January 10, I was reassigned to Camp S-122 in Boonville, NY. I was worried about Idaho but it was no problem to take him with me. We both boarded a train to New Jersey and then on to Booneville, New York by bus. Idaho seemed to enjoy the ride and the attention but then he was used to traveling all day long.

In Boonville, once again Idaho enjoyed trucking on a daily basis. We completed our tour and returned to Brockport, NY the first part of April 1936. By now he was still a puppy full of energy who could retrieve and run like crazy. He listened though and was loyal, always responding when called.[109]

DOG NUMBER 2

The second dog in this trial was Rex, dubbed by the media as the "alibi dog." Since Idaho was identified by numerous witnesses as the murder dog, Harry Sessions, Idaho's defense attorney, called in Rex, an Idaho look-alike, to try to cast doubt on the eyewitness identifications. At the trial, Sessions called for the "alibi dog," which was led in and placed on the table before the judge by his owner, Herbert Rose. Sessions questioned eyewitness Clem Snover.

Q. Did the other dog resemble this dog?
A. A little, but it's not the same one.[110]

Even though Sessions did not receive the exact answer he wanted, he was still able to instill some "reasonable doubt" in the courtroom that the dogs did have some similarities and that it was possible that, in the heat of the moment, a witness might not be able to recognize a look-alike.

DOG NUMBER 3

A third dog, "the kidnapped dog," entered the media mayhem when Giles Hoyt, chief of police in Brockport, received a telegraph message from E.L. Whitmore, chief of police in Moscow, Idaho. This new dog resulted in more newspaper headlines and a disagreement among three police agencies.

> *Dog accused of drowning boy answers description (stop)*
> *of animal stolen from Idaho Falls, Idaho. Hold dog (stop)*
> *until airmail description. (stop)*

This telegram and the follow-up letter resulted in a controversy among police agencies in the area regarding who had jurisdiction to investigate the missing dog. The day after the telegram arrived, the letter from Moscow, Idaho arrived with the address of Chief Hoyt of the Brockport Police Department crossed out and the address of the Rochester police chief penciled in. The letter did not stop there. The Rochester Police Department gave the letter to the Monroe County Sheriff's Office. Chief Hoyt demanded that the letter be returned to him.[111]

The description in the letter came from Carl W. Hosington, who thought he recognized Idaho's picture in the paper and asked Chief Whitmore to wire the Brockport officers. Hosington said he thought the dog was one reported lost or stolen last spring from his brother-in-law, Cecil R. Tulley, county agricultural agent in Idaho Falls.

Hosington went on to say that Tulley's dog was fond of water and used to ride his back while swimming. He said he also taught the dog to ride a surfboard and that it would often run and leap fifteen or twenty feet from the bank into the water. Hosington described the missing dog as half Pointer and half Irish Setter and playful as a puppy, although he was eight years old.[112]

After reading the description, Chief Hoyt settled the matter himself. The last paragraph from Hosington described a "pointer-Irish setter mix," and the missing dog was eight years old. Idaho was a German Shepherd–

Airedale mix and only nine months old. Hoyt did not need the Rochester Police Department or the Monroe County sheriff to investigate for him. Idaho was not the missing dog from Idaho.[113]

DOG NUMBER 4

During the two-week hiatus between the hearings and the trial, letters and donations rolled in supporting Idaho's defense. Idaho received a letter and a donation from a famous Hollywood dog, Kentucky Boy, who became the fourth dog associated with the trial.

> *My name is Kentucky Boy. I am just an Airedale dog—yet the governor of California, the Mayor of Los Angeles and many noted persons have conferred honors on me because I am credited with saving many lives and preventing the destruction by fire of a studio in Hollywood.*
>
> *I am now pleading for the life of Idaho and the dollar enclosed is my contribution for his defense. Sincerely yours, Kentucky Boy 3rd, 3814 Sunset Blvd. Hollywood, Calif.*

The letter was signed with the obligatory paw print.[114] Kentucky Boy was indeed famous. On August 15, 1929, a fire broke out at the Evans Studio in Hollywood, California. Kentucky Boy was out for a walk with his owner, Robert Byrne. As they walked along Hollywood Boulevard, the dog broke loose and started running toward the Evans Studio. By the time Byrne caught up to Kentucky Boy, the dog was barking at a door with smoke pouring out. Byrne sounded an alarm, help arrived and the fire was extinguished before significant damage was done to the structure, although some material inside was burned. The California Humane Society gave Kentucky Boy a medal; he won nineteen more medals and a number of product endorsements. Kentucky Boy was credited with saving three hundred people in a nearby theater.[115]

So, now there were four dogs involved in the trial: Idaho, the defendant; Rex, the alibi; the Idaho Falls "kidnapped dog"; and Kentucky Boy, Hollywood star and contributor to Idaho's defense fund. However, the canine chorus in support of Idaho continued when a fifth dog entered the picture.

Left: Kentucky Boy letter. *Reproduced by the author.*

Below: Kentucky Boy, Hollywood hero dog. *Reproduced by the author.*

Paddy Reilly begging for donations. *Reproduced by the author.*

Paddy Reilly medal. *Reproduced by the author.*

DOG NUMBER 5

Paddy Reilly, the mascot of the New York Humane Society, joined the letter writers to Judge Benedict. "As a dog who has saved many lives, both human and animal, I plead for fair play for Idaho."[116] During Paddy's six years as mascot, he was credited with saving a total of ten animals and forty people, including two drowning children. The irony here is that Paddy is credited with saving many swimmers from drowning, as portrayed in a Humane Society poster, while the Brockport trial was about a dog accused of causing a drowning. This trial was fast becoming a chorus of canine voices.

A SIGN OF THE TIMES

Brockport's famous "murder dog" trial is definitely an event that was a sign of the times. In 1936, it was difficult to find good news. The nation was still deep in the Depression, the unemployment rate stood at 16.9 percent and the tar-paper shacks of the homeless, called "Hoovervilles," still stood in many cities throughout the United States. The effects of such government programs as the Social Security Act (1932), the Civilian Conservation Corps (1933) and the Works Progress Administration (1935) were just beginning to be felt at this point. July 1936 was a slow news time, especially for good news.

What if the Brockport trial had happened in the early years of the decade? The Lindbergh kidnapping was worldwide news in 1932, and the investigation was followed closely from 1932 until Hauptmann's arrest in 1934. Hauptmann's trial began in January 1935 and quickly became a media circus. H.L. Mencken described it as "the biggest story since the Resurrection."[117] Thousands of spectators and hundreds of reporters and radio and telephone technicians overwhelmed Flemington, New Jersey. The largest telephone system ever assembled to that date for a single event was created—large enough for a city of one million.[118]

The trial itself lasted five weeks and called an endless array of witnesses and experts. Would the news services have paid any attention to a small-village dog trial when they had the 1932 kidnapping of Charles Lindbergh's son to write about? The search for the kidnapper/killer went on for two years between 1932 and 1934. Hauptmann's trial was even more sensational and had a worldwide audience right up through the appeals and subsequent execution of Hauptmann in the electric chair in April 1936, only three months before the Brockport trial. News crews from Paramount and the Associated Press would have had a far bigger event to cover than a dog trial in the Village of Brockport.[119]

So, how could a journalist compare the "trappings" of a five-day dog trial to the five-week "Trial of the Century"? The Brockport trial, like the Hauptmann trial, did turn into a media circus. The small town of Brockport and its Town Hall were overcrowded with spectators and media. The small town of Flemington, New Jersey (population 2,700), and the equally small Hunterdon County Courthouse were overrun with reporters, news crews, photographers and technicians. Both trials attracted more than their share of spectators. The circus atmosphere of the Hauptmann trial was enhanced by the selling of souvenirs—locks of the dead boy's hair and pieces of wood from the ladder used to reach the boy's bedroom. The Brockport trial inspired Idaho's plaster of Paris paw prints, selling for $100 a set. The prosecutor in the Brockport trial called a long list of witnesses and experts, as did the prosecutor in the Hauptmann trial. And the Brockport trial did attract national and some international attention. Both trials attracted publication offers. Victor Fortune refused book and movie offers. Anna Hauptmann, Bruno's wife, used that leverage to pay for a lawyer for her husband.[120]

Despite the description of the Brockport trial having all the trappings of the Hauptmann trial, the two trials were obviously not in the same league. One was on a very large stage, involving the kidnapping and murder of the son of an internationally known aviator, Charles Lindbergh. The other, on a much smaller stage, involved an unknown local dog. How did the "murder dog" trial come to attract so much attention?

From the April 1936 execution of Hauptmann to the beginning of August 1936 was a slow news time. It was during the recess in the Brockport trial, between the July 21 hearing and the August 5 trial, that the national news services took hold of this unusual event and ran with it. The break between the hearing and the trial gave this story momentum. There was little national or worldwide news to distract from the Brockport trial, and after all the Lindbergh news of the previous four years, the media needed another sensational story. What if the Brockport tragedy had happened two weeks later?

On the other hand, during the period that followed, August 3–9, there was plenty of news. African American athlete Jesse Owens won four gold medals at the Berlin Olympics in front of Adolf Hitler, who had recently begun his campaign for the "dominance" of the Aryan race. News of Owens's accomplishments sparked considerable public interest. The buildup to the Brockport trial began in the two-week period prior to the trial and before Owens hit the national headlines. By then, the nation was absorbed in the case and awaiting the outcome of the August 5 trial.

What if the Brockport "murder dog" trial had happened in the 1940s instead of the 1930s? War news, the atomic bomb and postwar happenings gave the media plenty to talk and write about. Would an incident concerning a dog and a small Upstate New York village have even been noticed? Despite rationing during the war years, prosperity returned, men left for the war, women went to work in factories and other wartime occupations and America had more important things to fill the news.

The Great Depression was a tremendous influence during the years before and after the trial in Brockport, New York. Aside from the scarcity of good news and the need for distraction, Brockport families and those of the rest of America were struggling to obtain the necessities of life. They were desperate to find jobs, clothing and food.

The Fortune family was a good example. Idaho's owner, Victor Fortune, was an unskilled, unemployed member of a family on government assistance. Victor's family included his mother, Ada Ives Fortune; his father, George; his younger brothers, Norman and Jack; and a sister, Doris. For years before the trial, Victor could find only part-time work. George lost his farm and store because of the Great Depression and was working only part-time. In Victor's own words, he describes the dire straits his family was in.

The year was 1933. My life was hard. I was 23 years old and couldn't find a job. My Mom and Dad had four children, lost their farm and grocery store because my Dad gave credit to people that were hungry. Consequently, we ended up in a really bad way. We were renting a home at 306 Holley Street in Brockport, New York. Dad was working for an area farmer but was hardly able to put food on the table. Mom would get defective cans of beans from the local cannery and the night I left home there was one can of beans to feed the entire family. I knew it was time to go off on my own.

The jobs I got usually only fed me for a couple of days and if I was lucky, I might get a place to sleep and a place to wash up. I slept outside a lot. I went hungry a lot. Life was hard. President Franklin D. Roosevelt created a program called the Civilian Conservation Corps. The next day I went to the village hall and enlisted. I was immediately accepted and provided travel to Ithaca, New York.[121]

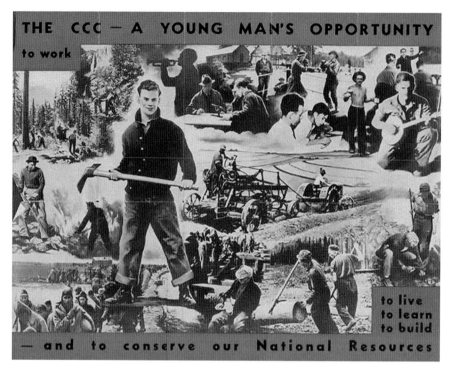

CCC poster. *Reproduced by the author.*

Despite the urgent need for the CCC, it is still remarkable that the time from its proposal to implementation was only three weeks. For those used to government bureaucracy, the legislation and implementation of the CCC were accomplished very quickly. Roosevelt made his request to Congress on March 21, 1933. The legislation was submitted to Congress the same day, and Congress passed it by voice vote on March 31. Roosevelt signed it the same day and issued an executive order on April 5 creating the agency. He appointed its director, Robert Fechner, and assigned War Department corps area commanders to begin enrollment. The first CCC enrollee was selected on April 8. For Victor Fortune, the CCC was all it was advertised to be. "It was a good deal. I received $25.00 a month for my parents, $5.00 per month for me, two pair of shoes, two sets of clothing and seasonal gear. Most of all, I got a place to sleep and all the food I could eat. I think it was my first pair of new shoes and clothes that fit!"[122]

Placing the U.S. Army in charge of the CCC was a brilliant move. It was already transporting recruits from all over the country to army bases anywhere in the country. The army was equipped to supply the men with food, clothing and housing. There are still men and women, fifty years after serving in the armed forces, who tell how well the uniforms fit. For years, they had put up with hand-me-down, ill-fitting clothes; those fortunate enough to buy new clothes who were not a standard size wore 32-length sleeves that were an inch too long or 30-inch sleeves that were too short. Men with a 31 inseam wore pants an inch too short or an inch too long. In the military, pants and shirts came in your size. The army was used to transporting, clothing, feeding and leading troops. Reserve officers were put in charge of CCC camps, but there was no military training.

Victor went to Ithaca, New York, to CCC Company 1254, Project SP-6, to clear land and build roads and trails in Enfield Park (now part of Robert H. Treman State Park), Buttermilk Falls Park and Taughannock Falls Park. Victor describes his early days with the CCC.

My intake was at the Borg Warner Building in Ithaca, New York. The big yellow building was located on one of the steepest hills and we were located in the newest part of the building where we were housed, had physicals and learned about our coming work.

I was assigned to Company 1254 which was located at Miller Field in Enfield, New York, just outside of Ithaca. Our Company became a team quite quickly and we were all pretty good friends. Our lodging was in tents that were built off the ground on wooden platforms. Sleeping quarters were pretty close but I didn't care. I had new shoes that fit, army gear, and three-square meals a day. The work was hard. We were clearing parkland, making roads throughout the park. We worked about eight hours a day, showered and got ready for dinner. Following supper, we would get together and teach each other things. Some guys worked on engines, some learned to read and that's where I learned to play the harmonica. Once I learned how to play, we would sit around and play music. Some of the members would sing. We'd laugh and go to town on weekends. The work was hard but it was a good life. I worked on Enfield Park, Buttermilk Falls and Taughannock Park.

While I was there, I learned to drive a truck. I became the chauffeur. I hauled the men to work, ran supplies, and worked. I loved to drive and became the go to guy if you needed anything.[123]

Roosevelt's plan worked just as he had described it in his initial address to Congress. The work the CCC did was designed to be unique and to not take away scarce, already existing jobs. It contributed not only to helping the

Above: Enfield Glen (Robert Treman Park, Ithaca, New York) postcard. *New York State Park Service.*

Left: CCC camp, Enfield Park, Ithaca, New York. *Photograph in author's collection.*

present financial situation during the Great Depression but also to benefit future financial gain for the nation.

> *I propose to create the CCC to be used in complex work, not interfering with normal employment and confining itself to forestry, the prevention of soil erosion, flood control, and similar projects. I call your attention to the fact that this type of work is of definite, practical value, not only through the*

prevention of great present financial loss but also as a means of creating future national wealth.[124]

The effect of Victor's enlistment in the CCC was felt at home almost immediately. The family's financial condition improved. Instead of a single can of beans for a family of six, Ada Fortune wrote to her son in September to describe a special birthday dinner for his brother Norman.

Sept. 21, 1933
We served tomato soup, roast pork with dressing, buttered beets, mashed potatoes with gravy, pickles and baked beans, warmed rolls, birthday cake with whipped cream, and cocoa.[125]

Even though this was a special birthday dinner, if other families fared as well, there were signs that the economy, at least on the local level, was beginning to improve a little bit. The first part of Roosevelt's plan was already showing results. Fewer people were starving, and more were able to afford food. The national economy was slower to respond, but the Fortunes

Victor Fortune driving CCC truck. *Photograph in author's collection.*

went from one can of beans for six people to a full-dinner birthday party for the family and Norman's Boy Scout friends, thanks to Victor's twenty-five dollars a month from the CCC.

The second part of Roosevelt's plan, "creating future national wealth," was prophetic. How many tourists now visit the parks that Victor's CCC company created? Today, Ithaca enjoys the economic and recreational benefits of Buttermilk Falls State Park, Enfield Park (Robert H. Treman State Park) and Taughannock Falls Park. Just read the promotion from Visitithaca.com: "Ithaca is Gorges! When traveling in New York, there is no better place to see beautiful waterfalls within such a small radius. With over 150 waterfalls including Taughannock Falls, Enfield Glen at Robert H. Treman State Park, Ithaca waterfalls are a must see!"[126]

Victor came back home after a year with the CCC, but the job situation had not improved much by 1934. Even though unemployment declined by 3 percent (from 24.75 percent in 1933 to 21.60 percent in 1934), there were still few jobs to be had. The CCC prepared him for a job, but the economy was still recovering, and despite new job skills and a great résumé, Victor found only frustration in his quest for employment. "Upon completion of my first year in the CCC's, I was excited to return to Brockport. I was sure I could get a job driving. I had great references from my CCC duty and my record was excellent. Things weren't much better in Brockport regarding work. I tried to work for nearly a year when I re-enlisted in the CCC's April 24th for another year-long stint."[127]

Victor was assigned to his old company in New York, but about halfway through the year, it was transferred to the state of Idaho. The camp was located just outside of Salmon, Idaho. It was in this camp that Victor cared for a litter of puppies and picked one out for himself. He named the puppy Idaho, and as soon as it was weaned from its mother, Queenie, Victor started taking the dog everywhere with him. He said that Idaho slept so close to him on the bed that he didn't have room for his feet. Before the year was up, the CCC company was transferred back to New York. This time, it was assigned to Camp S-122 in Boonville, an Adirondack camp.

On January 10, I was reassigned to Camp S-122 in Boonville NY. I was worried about Idaho but it was no problem to take him with me. We both boarded a train to New Jersey and then on to Boonville, New York by bus. Idaho seemed to enjoy the ride and the attention but then he was used to traveling all day long. In Boonville, once again Idaho enjoyed trucking on a daily basis. The Civilian Conservation Corps (CCC) had a camp (S-122) just east of Boonville, New York. The site lies within the Hogsback State Forest on the south side of Woodgate Road (County Road 61) leading to State Route 28, which runs across the Adirondack Park.

From this camp, the CCC "boys" carried out forestry projects around the west side of the park, such as planting trees, forest thinning, eradication of pests, and fire suppression. They built truck trails for firefighting around the hamlet of Otter Lake and reforested 1700 acres around Lyonsdale. Boys from this camp also built Pixley Falls State Park south of Boonville and helped with restocking streams with trout. We completed our tour and returned to Brockport, NY the first part of April 1936.[128]

Again, Roosevelt's prediction for the future benefits of the CCC rings true. Here is what the "I Love New York" promotion site has to say about Pixley Falls State Park, built by Victor's CCC crew in 1936: "Roughly an hour outside of the city of Syracuse and taking you up into Oneida County, Pixley Falls State Park is an underrated gem within our park system."[129] The Civilian Conservation Corps provided Victor with another year of employment and job training and New York State with a future tourist attraction.

When Victor returned in 1936, things were slightly better for the Fortunes. Victor's father, George, was now employed by the Works Progress Administration (WPA). George Fortune, along with William Breeze and other Brockport men, had just taken advantage of jobs with the WPA, established by Franklin D. Roosevelt on May 6, 1935.

The program provided employment developing infrastructure to support current and future society. The Works Progress Administration built, improved or renovated 39,370 schools, 2,550 hospitals, 1,074 libraries, 2,700 firehouses, 15,100 auditoriums, gymnasiums and recreational buildings, 1,050 airports, 500 water-treatment plants, 12,800 playgrounds, 900 swimming pools, 1,200 skating rinks and many other structures. It also dug more than 1,000 tunnels, surfaced 639,000 miles of roads and installed nearly 1,000,000 miles of sidewalks, curbs and street lighting. It also installed tens of thousands of viaducts, culverts and roadside drainage ditches.[130] The WPA hoped to end the Depression or alleviate its worst effects. It proved to be better than public assistance, because it maintained self-respect through work, reinforced the work ethic and kept up job skills. What George Fortune's particular job was is unknown. The job market was still tough, and Victor did what he could to help the family. "Upon my return to Brockport, I was still unemployed. I would do a little part-time work here and there driving

Depression-era man with sign. *Reproduced by the author.*

whenever possible. Small jobs didn't usually pay much but farmers would take me on for a day or two because they knew I'd show up if I took the job and that I would give a fair day's work for a fair day's wage. Back then it may have only been a dollar, but a dollar went a long way."[131]

Things were only slightly better for William Breeze's family and many others in the Village of Brockport. Anna Breeze was often referred to as an invalid. She used a wheelchair to get around and was rumored to have had polio as a child. Victor said that Max was devoted to his mother. "Maxwell Breeze was a really nice kid and his parents were nice people. His Dad William had immigrated to the United States from Canada when Max was about a year old. His Mom Anna was born in Rochester NY and married Willie in Toronto Canada. His Dad worked for the WPA just like my Dad. They had really struggled through the Great Depression. Max was only 14 and their only son."[132]

Maxwell Breeze was a well-liked and active member of many groups. On the day of the drowning, he was playing baseball with the Muckland Nine, a team that practiced and played numerous games in a youth league. Max was also active with the Boy Scouts, earning many awards and merit badges, as well as participating in overnight camping trips with his troop. He participated in school activities as a singer and actor in dramatic productions.[133] Only days after Max's death, Victor Fortune went from the ranks of the unemployed to employment with a Brockport canning company.

The other aspect of the Great Depression that may have had an effect on the notoriety of the Brockport "murder dog" trial was the recreation that people turned to for distraction. It centered on cost, because few people had the money to pay for entertainment. Radio was one of the free sources of Depression-era entertainment. Victor's mother mentioned listening to the radio and constantly hearing news about the impending trial. The trial news traveled far from Brockport, and columnist Albert Payson Terhune commented about hearing over the radio that he was testifying in the trial, when, in fact, he was at home, hundreds of miles from Brockport at that time. Every day in the local newspapers, long lists of radio stations and their programs took up an entire page. The listings included not only local stations but also stations that offered local reception. The radio programs broadcast twenty-four hours a day, seven days a week, and the page in the newspaper contained advertisements for specific stations and specific programs.[134] It was during this time that such programs as *The Jack Benny Program*, *The Eddie Cantor Show*, *Major Bowes' Original Amateur Hour*, *Lux Radio Theatre*, *The George Burns and Gracie Allen Show*, *Bing Crosby's Kraft Music Hall* and *Amos 'n' Andy* were heard on the radio, along with dozens of other weekly programs broadcast from New York City, Chicago and Los Angeles. Families would gather around the radio in the evening to hear their favorite shows. Kids gathered around the radio before supper to listen to *The Lone Ranger*, *The Green Hornet* and *Jack Armstrong, the All-American Boy*.

Movies were a great distraction for those who could afford them. It was common to see a Saturday double feature, along with cartoons, serials, a newsreel and a short subject. Brockport's Strand Theater, one of the oldest continuously operating movie theaters in the United States, supplied film entertainment during the Depression. The billboard in front of the Strand Theater shows some of the films offered to Brockport audiences in 1937.

Free entertainment may have been one reason that five hundred people came out on a hot summer's day to sit or stand in a crowded courtroom for five and a half hours. Arch Merrill of Rochester's *Democrat and Chronicle* called it "the most exciting day in Brockport history."[135] The Strand

Advertisement for radio stations. *Reproduced by the author.*

Strand Movie Theater, Brockport, New York. *Reproduced by the author.*

Strand movie posters. *Reproduced by the author.*

Theater was suggested as the location for the trial via a petition from a group of Brockport citizens. The trial seemed more like a theater event, with spectators laughing, applauding and even hissing. Judge Benedict warned the courtroom spectators on a number of occasions to refrain from these activities.

There is little doubt that the notoriety of the Brockport "murder dog" trial was a result of many factors: media sensationalism, lack of good news stories and the actions of the judge, defense attorney and spectators. In other words, many things came together to make these "the most exciting days in Brockport history."[136]

8

THE MURDER DOG TRIAL

Part 2

As the parade of witnesses continued, would there be any revelations to sway Judge Benedict one way or the other? What strategy would Harry Sessions employ for his remaining witnesses? What did he have up his sleeve for a final summation?

After the half-hour recess, Patrolman Henry Jensen of Rochester was called to the stand. He testified that, following the hearing and during the two-week examination of Idaho, the dog had been placed in the water with a swimmer and behaved perfectly, even when encouraged to play. Jensen received applause from the courtroom spectators that was immediately stopped by Judge Benedict.

Q. Do you recommend that the dog be killed?
A. No, Sir. I do not.[137]

Rochester *Times Union* reporter Justin Gagie took the stand and testified that Idaho showed no viciousness when swimming in the Erie Canal at Genesee Valley Park with Gagie. Gagie said that the experiment with Idaho lasted about thirty minutes. What did not come out at the trial was the description of that experience that Gagie wrote in an article, "Reporter Swims with 'Killer' Dog: Finds Him Playful, but Rough." Gagie goes on to say in that article, but not in his testimony at the trial, "Any person not an experienced swimmer, or one who loses his head and becomes frightened, could get into trouble with Idaho."[138] The reporter ends his article with the

Newsreel title slide. *Grinberg Paramount Pathe Inc., used with permission.*

following description on the outcome of his tussle in the canal with Idaho. "Thirty-seven scratches, counted by Officer Jensen when he applied the iodine, a glass cut on the left foot, and a refreshing dip, were my reward for the experience."[139]

The reporter's experience, observed by Dr. and Mrs. William Mahoney; Mary Foubister; Frank Graff of the Genesee Valley Park; Paul McNamara, a Harvard Law student; and patrolman Henry H. Jensen, was, of course, never completely entered into the court records. The three witnesses who did appear were asked only about general observations of Idaho's behavior in the water with a swimmer. As Victor had advised his family, they kept their answers brief and relevant to the specific questions asked by Harry Sessions. The witnesses were well-prepared.

The next witness was Mary Foubister, secretary of the Rochester Dog Protective Association. She said that she had examined ten thousand dogs in her official capacity.

> *Q. Did you examine Idaho?*
> *A. Yes.*

Foubister gave Idaho's breed as German Shepherd/Airedale and his age as nine months. She said Idaho weighed fifty pounds. Sessions continued with his questioning.

> Q. *Would you class him as a puppy?*
> A. *Yes.*
> Q. *How about his disposition?*
> A. *He's very lovable.*
> Q. *Is he dangerous?*
> A. *No.*
> Q. *Does he bite?*
> A. *No.*
> Q. *What about his conduct in the water?*
> A. *Very ordinary.*
> Q. *Do you think he should be killed as a vicious dog?*
> A. *I do not.*[140]

Gladys Richardson and Deputy Oren Tuttle were called to support the claim that Idaho was not dangerous. Next, a key witness, Dr. William H. Mahoney, a veterinarian from the Humane Society, was called and supported Mary Foubister's testimony. Dr. Mahoney reportedly went over the dog from head to tail. He also conducted a reenactment of the drowning by having Idaho in the canal with a swimmer. He also conducted observations on land to see if Idaho became overly excited during certain circumstances. Mahoney ran blood tests to ensure that the dog was not diseased. As a result, he offered the following testimony.

> Q. *Do you consider this dog, Idaho, a dangerous dog?*
> A. *I wouldn't say so.*
> Q. *Do you believe he's guilty of the murder of this boy?*
> A. *Not in any way.*
> Q. *In light of your experience, would you say this dog should be killed?*
> A. *No, Sir.*[141]

Helen Moser, witness number eighteen, and Mrs. George Hinman, witness number nineteen, served as character witnesses for the defense. Now, the prosecutor, James Costigan, called Donald Duff, fifteen, one of the boys with Maxwell Breeze when he went swimming in the canal. The film crew moved in to record the witness. Duff insisted that the dog involved in the drowning was Idaho.

Seated from left to right: Dr. William Mahoney, Justice Homer B. Benedict, Harry Sessions. *Grinberg Paramount Pathe Inc., used with permission.*

Sessions abruptly stood up and ordered that Idaho be lifted to the table. The movie camera moved in to obtain a close-up of Sessions as he addressed Donald Duff.

> *Q. And you say this looks like the dog?*
> *A. It is the dog.*

At that response, Sessions called Deputy Sheriff Tuttle to the stand. Tuttle testified that Duff originally told him he couldn't identify the dog. When Duff was recalled, some in the crowd hissed, and Costigan pointed this out to Justice Benedict, who said he was unaware of the hissing but that if anyone hissed, he or she would be escorted from the courtroom. Donald Duff refused to be shaken and stuck by his testimony.[142] "That is the dog I saw in the Erie Canal swimming the day and hour that Maxie was drowned. That is the dog that I saw attempt to crawl upon Maxie's back."[143]

James Costigan then called Dr. Estelle Gloh, Harry Weise Jr., Marcus Weise and Leo O'Brien. Leo O'Brien got a chuckle from the courtroom crowd when he used the nicknames of his friends, such as "Popeye," instead of their given names.[144]

Marjorie Royal of Rochester was next on the witness stand, followed by Paul Hamlin. Hamlin was the boy who had tried to save Maxwell Breeze. Hamlin repeated his original story about the events leading up to the drowning and said that the dog pawed at him but "didn't get on top of me." "Can you identify the dog?", Costigan asked him. "Yes," Hamlin answered and pointed to Idaho.[145] "The Eyes and Ears of the World" camera moved in for a close-up of Idaho asleep at Deputy Tuttle's feet.

There was one witness who was said to have given testimony in this case but never appeared. That was the national dog expert, Albert Payson Terhune. Terhune was at home in Wayne, New Jersey, on the day of the trial when he heard on the radio that he was in Brockport testifying in the "murder dog" trial. "I did not attend the trial. There was no need. I had nothing to add to what I had told Sessions and the reporters. Thus, it was an odd experience for me, while I was sitting at work here at Sunnybank one afternoon, to be told over the radio that I was testifying in Brockport, several hundred miles away, at that moment."[146]

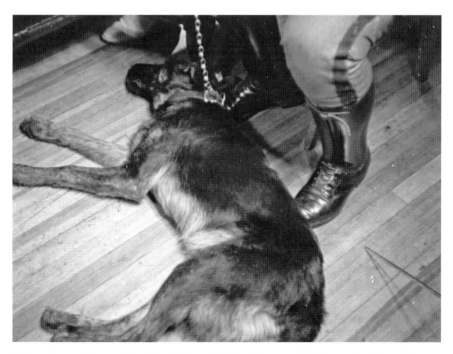

Idaho asleep at Deputy Oren Tuttle's feet. *Grinberg Paramount Pathe Inc., used with permission.*

It was now 2:30—twenty-seven witnesses and four and a half hours since the trial began at 10:00 a.m. Harry Sessions decided it was time to begin his summation. "Your Honor, the defense rests."

"You may begin your summation," Bendict directed.

> *My client, Your Honor, is only a mongrel dog who isn't worth $5. But people get attached to a dog in some way. I don't for a minute contend that this dog's life matches a boy's. I have the most respect for the feelings of the parents in this case and I want no one to misunderstand my point of view. But dogs are dogs. You wouldn't grow up without a dog, just an ordinary pup-dog. And I haven't heard a soul in the courtroom recommend that the dog be killed because, if this dog is dangerous, then every dog of the same age and breed ought to be killed. The best friend in this world that a man has may turn against him, but the one absolutely unselfish friend that a man can have in this selfish world is his dog. You know, it kind of gives you a glow around the heart.*[147]

"I know just how you feel. I have a dog myself," blurted out Justice Benedict.[148] Sessions ended his summation with a surprise recommendation that Idaho be taken from Brockport, where his presence would be a constant, painful reminder to the Breezes. But prosecutor Costigan had a surprise of his own. "I agree with Mr. Sessions that the dog should be confined," he said, as if he never wanted the death penalty after all. "But I don't agree

Paramount news camera. *Reproduced by the author.*

that he should be confined outside of Brockport. Idaho should be returned to Victor Fortune and confined by him."[149]

Judge Benedict took a brief recess to prepare his decision. This decision was different from any Homer Benedict had made in his thirty-four-year career. This time, unlike the many that never went beyond the confines of his law office, it would be broadcast on the radio and printed in newspapers coast to coast. Now, thousands waited for the verdict. Judge Benedict could take the advice of defense counsel and sentence Idaho to exile in a community other than Brockport. He could also consider the prosecution request to return Idaho to his owner, Victor Fortune, to be confined. If Idaho was to be confined, Judge Benedict had discretion as to the length of that confinement. It was possible for Benedict to declare Idaho a vicious or dangerous animal and impose the death sentence. Whatever the verdict, Benedict had the last word. His verdict could not be appealed. The Paramount camera moved in for a close-up of Judge Benedict as he delivered the verdict.

GUILTY OR NOT GUILTY

Justice Homer B. Benedict delivered his long-awaited verdict:

> *After considering the evidence in this case, I have decided that the actions of the dog, Idaho, while in the water, are dangerous, and that said subject, Victor Fortune, is hereby ordered to securely confine said dog from this date until October 1, 1938, and if said dog is not securely confined, any police officer or designated representative of the Commission of Farms and Markets is hereby ordered to kill said dog either on or off the premises.*[150]

Homer Benedict reached what he believed was a compromise. Idaho would be sentenced to death only if his owner failed to securely confine the dog for two years. For all his time and effort in conducting the hearing and trial, as well as dealing with the volumes of correspondence, Justice Benedict did not become a rich man as a result of the notoriety of the case. An article in the Poughkeepsie newspaper describes his compensation. "Homer Benedict, peace justice, who conducted the most publicized trial in recent western New York history, will receive $10.75 in fees for his work, the only public cost of the entire proceedings."[151]

As Judge Benedict slammed his gavel on the table announcing the end of the trial, Victor shook hands with Harry Sessions and expressed his reaction to the verdict that spared Idaho's life.

The scales of justice. *Reproduced by the author.*

Justice Benedict signing the court order sparing Idaho's life. *Grinberg Paramount Pathe Inc., used with permission.*

Victor Fortune shaking hands with Harry Sessions. *Grinberg Paramount Pathe Inc., used with permission.*

When the final judgment was read and Idaho was "sentenced to the chain"—I was relieved that he still had his life. I knew that no matter what, Idaho would stay on the chain and I was very lucky to still have him. I felt such gratitude to Harry and Mary for all they had done to keep Idaho safe and to help me spare his life. Harry was masterful during the cross examination, yet kind. There were so many people that were kind and helped, from those who raised money to those that knew and loved Idaho.

Everyone was shaking my hand and congratulating me. The cameras snapped pictures of Idaho and me. Mr. Breeze, however, just sat there. It was bittersweet. Few paid attention to Mr. Breeze and he left the court room. William Breeze just kept repeating, "It doesn't suit me."[152]

After the trial, the police took me home with Idaho sitting on the front seat. Idaho seemed to love it although the sirens were blasting. All those months of riding on the front seat of my truck with me had taught him to sit up straight. He loved a ride and this one was no different. People were actually waving!

Mary came over to the house along with my family and friends. We were all too tired to party much and Mary was taking Idaho to Canandaigua Lake for a couple of weeks for his safety. Idaho had a few people threaten to kill him and for his safety, I let him go with Mary. Mary truly loved Idaho. I went to visit them on the weekends and was glad when Idaho returned home. We were able to swim in the lake but I always kept him leashed when he was on shore. Although the sentence would not be enforceable in Canandaigua, I would take no chances with Idaho.[153]

William Breeze. *Grinberg Paramount Pathe Inc., used with permission.*

Maxwell Breeze's mother, Anna, who didn't attend the trial, was far more outspoken than her husband: "The people of Brockport have fallen pretty low when they place a dog's life above that of a child. If I had a gun, I would shoot the dog myself. My boy was all I had."[154]

In a letter to the United Press, she said: "My boy, Maxie, is dead, the victim of a dangerous mongrel dog. I believe that dog was Idaho, and I demand that he be killed. If the people of this country who are not parents continue, as they have in this case, to place the life of a mongrel dog above the life of a happy, healthy child, then it is time that all mothers give up the task of bringing up children."[155]

In response, Mary Foubister wrote:

> *I am not putting the life of a dog above that of a child when I ask that Idaho be allowed to live. For two weeks I have virtually lived with Idaho. I have observed his behavior in every conceivable situation—in water and on land. From my experience of 15 years with dogs of all breeds, I am convinced that Idaho is not vicious, not dangerous. His charts show him to be perfectly healthy and normal in every way.*[156]

Anna Breeze. *Grinberg Paramount Pathe Inc., used with permission.*

Interest in the trial did not end there. News articles mentioning the Brockport "murder dog" trial continued to appear years after the trial was over. It followed Victor Fortune for the rest of his life. Judge Benedict pronounced his verdict, and, as in most decisions, there were those who agreed and those who disagreed. Not only was the Village of Brockport divided; the entire country was also of two minds. Now, all these years later, without the media attention and the personal feelings of those involved, is the picture of what happened that July 21 and August 5 in 1936 any clearer?

In order to answer the question of whether Idaho was guilty or not guilty, we must ask another question: guilty or not guilty of what? Was Idaho guilty of murdering Maxwell Breeze? Was Idaho guilty of causing the drowning of Maxwell Breeze? Was Idaho guilty of attacking Daniel Houghton? Was Idaho even guilty of being in the canal on the days in question?

The first thing that comes through loud and clear is that this was not a trial to decide if Idaho was guilty of murder, but instead a hearing to determine if Idaho was a dangerous animal, based on a complaint by

Daniel Houghton. Judge Benedict ruled that Idaho was dangerous in the water. The judge was never charged with finding Idaho guilty or not guilty of murder in the drowning death of Maxwell Breeze.

This is where the purpose of the hearing and the trial became confused, along with the focus of the proceedings. Victor Fortune was prophetic when he said that Daniel Houghton's complaint would bring back speculation on Idaho's involvement in Maxwell Breeze's death. The first witnesses called were the boys present when Maxwell drowned on July 4. Judge Benedict himself started his questioning at the hearing by asking Donald Duff about Maxwell's drowning. The next group of witnesses gave testimony about Idaho's disposition and events on the day of the drowning and ignored the alleged attack on Daniel Houghton. The Houghton attack had no witnesses. It was strictly his word against the Fortune family's that Idaho was always at home. By the time of the trial on August 5, the testimony in the courtroom and the reporting by the media had shifted the focus of the trial from Daniel Houghton's original complaint to the drowning of Maxwell Breeze. There seemed to be no end to the publication of false information. "Idaho was charged with having attacked 14-year-old Russell Breese [*sic*] while the boy was swimming in the Barge Canal. He forced the boy under, his accuser said, drowning him. The boy's parents brought a civil suit to require the dog's owner to show cause why Idaho should not be destroyed as a vicious dog. Then followed a proceeding that was actually a murder trial with Idaho as the defendant."[157]

Here we have the whole story. All of it is incorrect, of course. The first sentence has Idaho charged with attacking the wrong person. From there, it goes on to misspell Max's name, wrongly claim that the trial resulted from a civil suit brought by the parents, falsely report that the result was "actually a murder trial" and end by identifying the wrong defendant. It is difficult, even now, to decide which came first, the media headlines proclaiming a dog on trial for murdering a boy, or a judge and lawyer conducting a trial of a dog for murdering a boy. A lone voice of reason in all of this came from a local newspaper reporter for the *Democrat and Chronicle* who questioned the propriety of the proceedings:

> *The phenomenon of the prosecution outdistancing the defense in leniency pleas climaxed a day of parliamentarian peculiarities which included the failure of the plaintiff (Daniel Houghton) to take the stand.*
>
> *The proceedings were brought by Daniel Houghton, 21, Brockport, after he was alleged to have been attacked July 11 and 14 in the Barge Canal*

by Idaho. Idaho, however, was tried strictly on evidence surrounding the drowning of Maxwell Breeze, 14-year-old Brockport high school boy, July 4 in the canal after being attacked by a mongrel.[158]

Even some of the testimony offered at the trial is suspect. How reliable are the identifications of Idaho and Rex, the alibi dog, when one of the dogs is tethered to a deputy sheriff? In another dog trial, in 1921, five dogs were brought into court, and the witness identified the murder dog. The judge threw out the identification of the dog because, of the five dogs, only one was held on a leash by a police officer.[159]

It is a matter of law beyond the scope of this book whether the Maxwell Breeze drowning should have been allowed into testimony at all, since no one was ever charged in that incident and the trial was supposed to be decided solely on the basis of the Houghton complaint. In the trial, Houghton's complaint was never verified by testimony from the plaintiff, eyewitnesses or medical reports, and it became secondary to the attention devoted to Maxwell.

There is also the question of why Harry Sessions, who bent over backward to prepare for the trial, did not object to testimony not relating to Daniel Houghton's original complaint. It was almost as if Sessions himself prepared for the trial assuming it would be about the drowning of Maxwell Breeze. It is one more mystery about this event that a newspaper reporter could see the "procedural peculiarities" and a judge and lawyer could not.

So, was Idaho guilty of causing the death of Russell Maxwell Breeze? Here, of course, there were people on both sides of this question. Many witnesses agreed that Idaho was not a vicious dog, but that does not answer the question of whether he was responsible for Maxwell's drowning. The witness with the closest look at the dog in the canal was Paul Hamlin, who had to fight off the dog and saw him face-to-face. Also, Hamlin's testimony of the dog climbing on the swimmer's back is supported not only by Donald Duff but also by Victor Fortune's own description of playing with Idaho in the water. "Friends would meet up by the Third Bridge which was a short walk from the house. As the water in the canal warmed, Idaho learned to swim with me. Oh, how he loved that. Everyone loved to watch us. He'd climb up on my back and jump. He loved our swim time and play."[160]

Three things stand out in Victor's statement: (1) swimming at the Third Bridge; (2) the short walk from the house; and (3) "He'd climb up on my back." All three of these statements match what was reported and testified to about the drowning. Maxie Breeze and the other boys walked to the Third

Bridge from the baseball field on Holley Street. The baseball field was in sight of the Fortune house, which was at 306 Holley Street. (The bridge was only "a short walk from the house.") Not only might Idaho have seen the boys as they walked along the canal behind the houses and followed them, but it was also only a short walk from where the incident occurred. George Fortune, Victor's father, testified in court that he saw the boys leave the ball field on July 4.

Idaho's playfulness in the water, which Victor describes, fits not only the description of the dog climbing on Max's shoulders but also Idaho's attempt to climb on Paul Hamlin, Daniel Houghton and Justin Gagie. It also fits with footage from the Paramount newsreel. The scene from the newsreel of the man in the water with Idaho was not seen by the participants in the trial until it was shown in movie theaters weeks later. It would have been valuable evidence for the prosecution that the drowning took place exactly as described by the boys accompanying Maxie that day and later by Paul Houghton. In the newsreel scene, as the man neared the middle of the canal, Idaho caught up to him and placed his paws over his shoulders. The man remained calm, but it was obvious in the film clip that the dog impaired his ability to swim. He appears to go under water for a moment.

Also, there is an identical description by the *Times Union* newspaper reporter Justin Gagie, who interacted in the canal with Idaho in front of five witnesses. He described difficulty dealing with Idaho and receiving numerous scratches as the dog attempted to climb on him. Although only nine months old, Idaho weighed fifty pounds. An experienced adult swimmer may have been able to take the evasive actions suggested by Albert Payson Terhune, but a fourteen-year-old, inexperienced swimmer was a different matter. It is difficult to understand Mary Foubister's testimony that Idaho behaved "normally" in the water.

It definitely seems possible that Victor's parents, who were watching Idaho for him while he was at a picnic at Hamlin Beach, were not as observant as they claimed. Idaho might not have been on the porch the entire day as Victor's father and brothers testified in court. He could have been hiding under the bed for fear of fireworks in the neighborhood, or, because their house was "only a short walk" to Third Bridge, they may have lost track of him for the brief period of time it took for this incident to take place.

One question never answered in the hearing or the trial was, Why were two swimmers scratched during their encounters with the dog and the other two not? That was a part of the testimony in the trial not explored beyond a simple yes-or-no question. The lack of scratches on Maxwell Breeze and Paul

Swimmer in Erie Canal with Idaho. *Grinberg Paramount Pathe Inc., used with permission.*

Idaho on swimmer in the Erie Canal. *Grinberg Paramount Pathe Inc., used with permission.*

Hamlin, and the multiple scratches on Daniel Houghton and Justin Gagie, would seem to be a natural path to pursue. Two witnesses, William Brady and Walter Welch, both testified that Max Breeze was not scratched. Albert Payson Terhune went into great detail about the difference between the claws on a cat and the nails on a dog. He said a dog could scratch someone but not dig the claws in like talons. Terhune may have been correct about that, but it does not explain the lack of scratches on two boys who encountered the dog in the water and those on Daniel Houghton and Justin Gagie. The lack or presence of scratches brings up three important questions: (1) How much interference did the dog in question cause?; (2) Was the encounter playful or vicious?; (3) Did the same dog attack all four swimmers? The difference could be used to claim the harmlessness of the contact between the dog and Paul and Max. It could also be used to cast doubt on whether all of the attacks were by the same dog, a tactic Harry Sessions may have had in mind with his initial question but one that was never followed up. It remains a mysterious inconsistency.

One last comment on the subject came, somewhat hesitantly, from Victor's daughter, who said that very shortly before her father died, she asked him if he had ever considered that Idaho was the dog who caused Maxwell Breeze's death. Victor told her that he never wanted to believe it but that he had some doubts about his mother's version of the story, because she blamed herself for not watching his dog closely enough and she had such compassion for all living things. "She loved animals. She'd barely kill a bug. One day she caught a queen bee and held it in her hand and it never stung her!"[161] Victor describes the reaction when he returned home on the day of the drowning. "Upon arrival home, my parents were horrified and my brother Jack, age 10, was extremely upset. They all said Idaho had never left the yard. He'd played at home all afternoon. He was not wet. He did not go away. Mom said when he wasn't playing, he was in the house under the bed because he was so afraid of the firecrackers that were going off."[162]

Was Idaho guilty of murder? Definitely not. That was never the question to be answered by the court of law. The boys at the beginning of the Paramount newsreel may have gotten it right, even before the trial started.

> *1ˢᵗ boy: Do you think the dog Idaho is responsible for Maxie's death?*
> *2ⁿᵈ boy: He was responsible for the drowning, but every dog likes to play like that and I don't think that he should die. He was just playing with Max out there in the water.*[163]

The irony is that this "trial" was never about the drowning of Russell Maxwell Breeze. The "summons," or "notice" for Victor Fortune to appear on July 21, 1936, and subsequently on August 5, 1936, was to answer a charge filed by Daniel Houghton after he claimed to have been "attacked" twice by Idaho while swimming. The judgement filed, after the "trial" on August 5, was a finding labeling Idaho a "dangerous dog in the water" for the attack on Houghton. Victor said it best after he was served with the court papers: "The hearing on the 21st was solely based on Daniel's charges but it opened up Max's tragic drowning."[164] The media and the public assumed that this case was about Max. The truth is that no charges were ever filed in the drowning death of Maxwell Breeze.

A TALE OF TWO TRIALS

Animal trials did not end in the eighteenth century or even in the nineteenth century. The last animal prosecution that Evans cites in *The Criminal Prosecution and Capital Punishment of Animals* occurred on May 4, 1906, the same year the book was published. Animal trials continued into the twentieth and twenty-first centuries. Jen Girgen pointed out the parallel between dangerous dog proceedings today and the old criminal trials of domestic animals.[165] When an animal attacks a human being, a legal ritual of hearing arguments for and against killing the offender takes place. The focus today is on preventing further injury rather than punishing a transgression. Modern-day dog trials that happened after the 1936 Brockport trial demonstrate the continuing practice of placing dogs on trial for offenses such as bites, attacks on other animals or the killing of a human being.

> *Nevertheless, the skeptic might insist these anecdotes are simply interesting oddities from the early part of the twentieth century, and that we would no longer prosecute and punish a nonhuman animal. To the contrary, evidence shows that despite the skeptic's protests, our modern criminal justice system still regularly holds animals responsible for their "offenses." Dogs, especially, frequently still find themselves in the position of defendant in modern American legal proceedings. Consider, for example, the laws mandating the execution of "vicious" dogs, which can set the stage for modern animal trials.*[166]

Before looking at two trials that came before the Brockport trial and may have had a direct influence on it, it may be enlightening to examine a few dog trials that came after. Many similarities exist between the Brockport "murder dog" trial and the dog trials leading into the twenty-first century. The trials followed strict legal protocol, heard testimony from witnesses and experts, drew large crowds of courtroom spectators, attracted local and national media attention and saw the influence of public opinion on some part of their outcome.

Fifty years after the Brockport trial, in 1984, an Old English Sheepdog named Champion Daralin Talisman's King Boots (Boots or Bootsie to family and friends) was accused of killing eighty-seven-year-old Gertrude Monroe in the home of his owners, Kathryn and Charles Schwarb, Gertrude Monroe's daughter and son-in-law. Boots, a veteran of hundreds of dog shows, had been before judges many times and always impressed them. But now Boots went on trial for his life before a judge in a court of law. Boots faced execution as a vicious animal in a much-publicized trial that attracted a great deal of attention in the wealthy Detroit suburb of Birmingham. The Schwarbs spared no effort or expense to save their dog.[167]

According to police reports, the 110-pound murder suspect was sleeping in a hallway when 97-pound Mrs. Monroe, frail and unsteady, staggered and toppled over on him. Jolted awake by the impact, Boots reacted by biting Monroe and inflicting wounds to the skull, face and neck. Mrs. Schwarb testified that she pulled the dog away and called the police, but her mother was pronounced dead soon after arriving at the hospital. The police arrested Boots for murder. The coroner's report stated that the bite on the back of the neck almost severed the spinal column. The Schwarbs insisted that Boots was only defending himself according to his instincts. They said Monroe had previously suffered several minor strokes and that she made no sound during the tussle with Boots. They claimed that another stroke or heart attack caused her to fall. "It wasn't the dog that killed her mother," argued the Schwarbs' attorney, Richard Selik. "She was dead when she hit the floor."[168]

There were differing conclusions from two autopsies. Oakland County medical examiner Dr. Bill Brooks testified that his examination of Mrs. Monroe's body "conclusively demonstrated at least six separate and distinct bites,"[169] indicating the dog continued to attack her after she fell on him. Dr. Henry Kallet, a professor of pathology at the University of Michigan Medical School, was hired by the Schwarbs to perform a second autopsy. Dr. Kallet told the court that Monroe's injuries were caused by a single bite. He also found a blood clot in her heart, which he said pointed to heart attack as the cause of death.[170]

Unlike the Brockport trial, testimony went on in a crowded courtroom, without Boots, who remained confined to the dog pound. Much like the Brockport trial, Boots had his fans who wanted to see him saved. Mail began to pour in and was almost 95 percent in the dog's favor. "People get out on bail every day, but this poor dog has been kept behind bars since the day he was placed there," protested local breeder Judy Crane. "It's a hard-enough time for these people, with everything that's happened. They shouldn't lose Boots too."[171]

At the conclusion of the trial, District Judge Edward Sosnick ruled that the dog was vicious. He ordered Boots destroyed by lethal injection unless his owners agreed to confine him at home for the rest of his days after having a veterinarian neuter him and pull his offending teeth. "I have to try to reason this out," said owner Kathryn Schwarb. "I'm so shaken I can't make up my mind."[172]

Boots's master witnessed the whole thing and, in spite of the special circumstances, when the dog was not only suddenly surprised but also may have believed he was being attacked, a judge still ruled that Boots was "vicious." The judge did give the Schwarbs two choices: Boots's death or confinement. They chose the latter option.[173]

Almost a decade later, the case of a New Jersey dog named Taro, who became a media sensation in the 1990s, has similarities with previous animal trials. The most famous of all "death row" dog cases involved Taro, a three-year-old Japanese Akita who was condemned to die under New Jersey's vicious dog law and held on "death row" for nearly four years. In 1991, Taro was seized by Bergen County officials after allegedly biting his master's ten-year-old niece. Then came a series of conflicting statements from local and national authorities, family and medical experts.[174]

Although local authorities claimed that Taro bit the girl, family members said the dog's paw caused the lip injury after the girl provoked the dog. At the hearing to determine if the dog was a vicious animal, a surgeon who treated the child after the attack testified that 15 to 20 percent of the child's lip was removed and that the injury was caused by a bite. Another doctor testified that the wound to the lip was most likely a result of a scrape.[175]

However, Taro had a prior record. Taro reportedly attacked three other dogs, killing one of them that was tied in her backyard at the time of the attack. On February 11, 1991, the battle to save Taro's life began after the judge ordered that Taro be killed. Taro's owners appealed the death sentence, and the county health department ordered that Taro be held in jail until judges decided whether he would be killed. The press called Taro New Jersey's "death row dog," and the story became national news. From March 1991 until February 10, 1994, Taro was held with German Shepherds in the Bergen County Sheriff's K-9 Unit as his case was debated in the New Jersey courts and legislature.[176]

In a letter that mirrored one written to Judge Benedict in the Brockport trial, a Haworth resident expressed her displeasure with the length of the appeals process. "It's all so absurd....You've got hardened criminals getting out on rape and robbery in less time than the dog's been in jail."[177] A break came on January 29, 1994, when Taro's case and photo made the front page of the *New York Times*. Taro had spent more than one thousand days as a prisoner, longer than the confinement of Idaho after the Brockport trial. Once again, public opinion contributed to the outcome. French actress Brigitte Bardot, in the manner of Irene Castle in the Brockport trial, among hundreds of dog lovers, weighed in with her support. Taro's tale was told on numerous television tabloid shows, and numerous attempts were made in the New Jersey legislature to introduce bills granting the Akita his freedom.[178]

Taro's case even spanned two New Jersey governors. Finally, pressure from the New Jersey legislator who introduced the bill that Taro was tried under, as well as public outcry, convinced the present governor, Christine Todd Whitman, to pardon Taro but ban him from the state of New Jersey. It was another case in which public opinion swayed justice in favor of the offending animal.[179]

But wait, Taro's case did not end there, because the residents of a town in New York State, where Taro was reported to be living, petitioned the governor of New York. "The Village of Pleasantville recently passed a resolution asking Gov. Mario M. Cuomo (New York) to convey to Governor Whitman (New Jersey) the village's strenuous objection to the terms of the 'pardon' granted to the owners of the dog Taro."[180] Taro's case was starting to resemble a Racine comedy. But it was hardly humorous to Taro and his owners.

Another trial, in Oregon in the 1990s, involved Nadas, a Malamute-Collie mix. Nadas was ordered to be euthanized after a neighbor claimed that the dog had chased her horse. The publicity and notoriety associated with Nadas was similar to that of Taro in the New Jersey case. Nadas's case also ended with the commutation of the lucky dog's death sentence in exchange for an agreement by its owner to send the dog out of state.[181] There is no record if the people in the state where Nadas ended up ever complained to their governor.

For those who have difficulty believing that medieval courts sentenced a dog to death for killing a capon, this 1990s case is a modern version of the same thing. A five-year-old black Labrador mix named Prince made national news after he was sentenced to death for killing a rooster. Prince escaped from his yard and killed a rooster. Because of the attack, he was declared "vicious." Under Portsmouth, New Hampshire's vicious dog law, "vicious" dogs are always supposed to be kept restrained. After Prince escaped from his yard two more times, he was condemned to death under the town's "three-strikes-and-you're-out" ordinance for dogs deemed vicious.

Prince, however, lived a charmed life, because the executioner (the veterinarian at the animal hospital where Prince was being held) refused to carry out the sentence. In the meantime, as in Taro's case, the town police department and the mayor's office were flooded with letters and phone calls protesting Prince's sentence. In February 1997, the city agreed not to execute the dog if his owner agreed to find a new home for the dog outside of Portsmouth. There is no record of any objection raised by the people among whom this "vicious" dog was placed.[182] In the Brockport trial, it was suggested that Idaho be placed outside of Brockport.

The cases of Boots, Taro, Nadas and Prince are all reflections of the animal trials of earlier centuries and are related to the Brockport trial by the attempt at due process, the amount of media attention they attracted, the reaction of the public and some similarity in terms of sentencing the dog to confinement or exile. Essentially, the Brockport trial achieved the same result as the Boots and Taro trials. All of the dogs were allowed their freedom if they were removed from the locales where they were tried. In Idaho's case, Judge Benedict admitted that his sentence would not apply if Idaho was removed from Brockport. "Fortune is perfectly free to give him away," he said.[183]

FORMAL ANIMAL "TRIALS" ARE now rare (indeed, it is for this very reason that they are newsworthy). The accused animals received some form of due process and were permitted to live, primarily because their cases received so much media attention and an outpouring of public opinion. Although these more recent trials reveal some similarities to Brockport's trial, they serve to demonstrate that animals continue to be prosecuted into the twenty-first century.

This brings us to two earlier trials, one from the nineteenth century and another from the early twentieth century, with much closer ties to the

Brockport "murder dog" trial. In fact, similarities suggest that they may have directly influenced the Brockport trial. An 1870 trial about a dog, Old Drum, has many similarities to the Brockport case. In 1921, a dog was put on trial in a case that had an almost unbelievable number of similarities to that in Brockport.

In San Francisco, in 1921, Dormie, the dog on trial, had a lawyer, children contributed pennies for the dog's defense, letters were written to the judge, newspapers across the country carried the story, "alibi dogs" were brought in to try to confuse the eyewitnesses and character witnesses gave testimony in court. If ever there was a precedent set for the Idaho trial, this was it. The case was described in much the same way as the Idaho trial: "one of the weirdest trials in U.S. history."[184]

Dormie went on trial with his life at stake. Three differences with the Brockport trial are immediately notable: (1) Dormie received a trial by jury; (2) Dormie was accused of killing fourteen cats; and (3) Dormie was a purebred Airedale with a rich owner. However, it is the similarities between the two trials that stand out.

In the San Francisco trial, Dormie was picked out of a canine lineup of not one but five neighborhood dogs by the owner of one of the cats, Marjorie Ingals. In the Brockport trial, Idaho was identified by Donald Duff after an "alibi dog" was brought in to test his eyewitness testimony. However, in Dormie's trial, the judge threw out the eyewitness identification; the lineup was flawed by the fact that one of the dogs was being held on a leash by a police officer.[185] Harry Sessions missed that part of the trial record, because a similar situation existed in the Brockport trial. Idaho was in court on a leash held by a police officer when Rex was brought into court by his owner. Justice Benedict had no trouble with that.

Headlines about the Dormie trial appeared in newspapers across the country. The San Francisco trial had articles in the *Seattle Star*, the *Washington Times*, the *Jasper Weekly Courier* and other newspapers in a variety of states. Headlines about the Idaho trial appeared in newspapers from New York to California, and, just like the Dormie case, there were letters written to the judge and the newspapers.

The *Washington Times* ran a letter from a concerned citizen named Harold A. Isreal, who sarcastically claimed that the "trial would scare future criminals from committing crimes."[186] That should sound familiar to the letter written to Judge Benedict from "an admirer of dogs, Albany, NY." That letter writer said the trial "should be a warning to gangsters and criminals at large throughout the land."[187]

The *Chicago Tribune* was equally as sarcastic in its statement that the trial would "expose the inner secrets of the upper strata of dogdom,"[188] a reference to the Airedale's wealthy owner. The owner was most likely a golfer, because Dormie's name comes from a golf term that refers to the number of holes a golfer leads by and the number of holes left to play (for example, a three-hole lead with three holes left to play—or, in Dormie's case, three cats down with three cats to go). What happened next is almost identical to a statement that could be made about Idaho's trial. "The trial started and the courtroom was absolutely packed. As it turns out, Dormie was a very popular dog around town, and a multitude of children turned out to witness the proceedings. The kids were so invested in Dormie's case that they actually took up a collection to pay for his legal expenses."[189]

Other similarities include an insinuation that the judge was sympathetic toward dogs because he himself owned a dog. In Idaho's case, Judge Benedict uttered the statement, "I know just how you feel. I have a dog myself."[190] In the Dormie case, a journalist suggested, "Perhaps the judge had an Airedale of his own back home."[191] The breed of dog has some similarities in both trials. In the San Francisco trial, Dormie was an Airedale; in Idaho's case, he was part Airedale. In a coincidence, the Brockport hearing was on the twenty-first day of the month; the San Francisco trial took place on the twenty-first day of the month.

A *Psychology Today* article, "A Landmark Case for the Legal Rights of Dogs,"[192] suggests that the San Francisco trial may have set some legal precedents, such as, (1) Dogs have a legal right to a trial; (2) Dogs have the right to call character witnesses to testify as to their general reputation and disposition; and (3) A dog can demand to be identified as the specific dog in any designated violation. It even concludes: "A court case, which, following the usual legal practice of ruling in accord with precedents from earlier court decisions, could serve to redefine the rights of all dogs brought before the law." "Someday a lawyer might point back to 1921 and use Dormie's case as a way to get another killer canine off the hook."[193]

Did Mary Foubister or Harry Sessions know about the 1921 trial? Did Sessions use Dormie's case to get another "killer canine off the hook"? Sessions used most of the tactics from the San Francisco trial to save Idaho's life. The Dormie trial ended in a hung jury, and Dormie went free.[194] Idaho was tried before a judge, but his life was spared, and an eventual pardon was granted that set him free.

The 1921 trial involved a dog killing other animals. The other case, which took place in 1870, concerned a farmer who killed a dog. How do these cases relate to the Brockport trial? Neither of these cases was about the taking of a human life. Idaho was not charged with taking a human life, either. Idaho was on trial for his life for allegedly attacking Daniel Houghton, who survived his encounter with the dog.

The next dog trial has not only strong connections to Idaho's trial but also a place in the hearts of all dog lovers. The Old Drum trial took place in Warrensburg, Missouri, in 1870. Old Drum was a favorite hunting dog and was not present at the trial. He had been shot by a neighboring farmer's hired hand. Even though the Old Drum and Idaho trials differed in some respects, they had more similarities than differences. The 1870 trial's connection to the Brockport case seems undeniable. Both trials attracted attention far beyond their local roots. The two trials also involved strong feelings for both dogs, Idaho and Old Drum, and divided the community. In both trials, the courtroom was crowded with lawyers, witnesses, supporters on both sides, the press and the merely curious, seemingly far beyond what should have been the case for what appeared to be a simple local hearing.

The nineteenth century may seem like the distant past to twenty-first-century readers, but, in 1936, the two trials were only sixty-six years apart. It is very possible that Harry Sessions studied the famous summation from the Old Drum trial in law school or found it in his preparation for the Brockport trial.

Just about everyone has heard the old saying "A dog is man's best friend," or some variation of that phrase. It can be found in the transcript of the 1870 trial, and it was part of "one of the most memorable closing arguments ever made by a lawyer."[195]

Harry Sessions's tour de force may well have been his closing argument in Idaho's defense. His summation is reminiscent of the 1870 dog trial, in which the lawyer for the defense gave a closing argument that did not mention any of the testimony in the case but played on the emotions of the jury. It does not seem possible that Sessions was unaware of that 1870 trial, in which Senator George Graham Vest delivered the closing argument that "is one of the most enduring and passionate bits of prose to come out of a court proceeding" and would produce the saying, "a dog is man's best friend."[196] It is worth quoting in its entirety here.

Gentlemen of the Jury: The best friend a man has in this world may turn against him and become his enemy. His son or daughter that he has reared with loving care may prove ungrateful. Those who are nearest and dearest to us, those whom we trust with our happiness and our good name, may

Old Drum statue. *Reproduced by the author.*

become traitors to their faith. The money that a man has he may lose. It flies away from him perhaps when he needs it most. A man's reputation may be sacrificed in a moment of ill-considered action. The people who are prone to fall on their knees to do us honor when success is with us, may be the first to throw the stones of malice when failure settles its cloud upon our heads. The one absolutely unselfish friend that a man can have in this selfish world, the one that never deserts him, the one that never proves ungrateful or treacherous, is his dog.

Gentlemen of the jury, a man's dog stands by him in prosperity and in poverty, in health and in sickness. He will sleep on the cold ground where the wintry winds blow and the snow drives fierce, if only he may be near his master's side. He will kiss the hand that has no food to offer; he will lick the wounds and sores that come from encounter with the roughness of the world. He guards the sleep of his pauper master as if he were a prince. When all other friends desert, he remains. When riches take wing and reputation falls to pieces, he is as constant in his love as the sun in its journey through the heavens.

If fortune drives the master forth an outcast in the world, friendless and homeless, the faithful dog asks no higher privilege than that of his company to guard against danger, to fight against his enemies. And when the last scene of all comes, and death takes the master in his embrace and his body is laid away in the cold ground, no matter if all other friends pursue their way, there by his graveside will the noble dog be found, his head between his paws, his eyes sad but open in alert watchfulness, faithful and true even in death.[197]

With all of these similarities between two dog trials, it seems obvious that Harry Sessions went above and beyond in his preparations in Idaho's defense to include precedent-setting dog trials from the past. The proof that Harry knew of this trial is contained in an article about his summation in the *New York Times.* "The lawyer (Harry Sessions) quoted a former Senator whose exact name he'd forgotten."[198] That senator was one of the lawyers in the famous "Old Drum" trial, George Vest. Despite the fact that Sessions could not recall his name, he certainly could recall Vest's summation. That

Victor Fortune hugging "Man's Best Friend." *Grinberg Paramount Pathe Inc., used with permission.*

1870 trial was made into a movie in 2000, *The Trial of Old Drum*, and the word-for-word, final summation is delivered at the end of the film.

Sessions, like Vest, closed his defense with an equally emotional summation. Sessions had his own "a dog is man's best friend" closer that contains a direct quote from Vest's summation: "'The best friend in this world that a man has may turn against him, but the one absolutely unselfish friend that a man can have in this selfish world is his dog.'[199] You know that kind of gives you a glow around the heart."

And, with that summation, Victor Fortune had his best friend.

EPILOGUE

After the verdict was handed down, Victor Fortune did give Idaho to Mary Foubister for a week. Both Mary and Victor were concerned, because Idaho had received death threats. Mary took Idaho to Canandaigua Lake for a "vacation." After that, Victor hoped to get back to a normal life. But life was hardly normal. Victor and Idaho still had more work to do to pay debts incurred by the trial.

> *Paramount sent in photographers and story writers. We did a few paw prints of Idaho's front paws out of Plaster of Paris and sold a few for $100.00. I never kept any. I wish I had. We needed the money so the sets Mary made, we sold*
>
> *The Friday after the trial I met with Harry to discuss a deal with Paramount. We were already scheduled to do more stints at Loew's in Rochester. The money that we made at Loew's would pay all the legal bills that we had as well as something for Harry. Idaho and I simply walked on stage, spoke of the trial and did a few tricks. I only did this so I could pay Harry and make a donation to the Rochester Animal Shelter that took care of Idaho. Harry tried to convince me to work with Paramount and their authors. The money was more than I could have ever imagined. I looked at Harry and said, "I can't do it to the Breeze Family. I can't make money based on the loss of a child. I will only do this until my debts are paid." Idaho and I went on stage. It was easy and the people loved it. The week ended. I hoped we could go back to a normal life.* [200]

The news media would not let the Hollywood angle die. The *Ithaca Journal* published a headline, "Dog May Get Chance in Films," and a story that reported, "His owner, Victor Fortune, is considering offers."[201] This article describing the theater appearance was published in a local paper on August 14, 1936:

> *Idaho the much-publicized dog acquitted of drowning a boy in the nearby Erie Canal, yesterday was launched on a stage career. The puppy, already a seasoned performer before movie cameras, began a week's personal appearance engagement at a local theater with his owner, Victor Fortune. A few remarks by Fortune plus Idaho's limited store of tricks, shaking hands and barking for a morsel to eat, comprised their routine. Fortune would not indicate if a more extensive stage career is in store for his dog, Idaho, sentenced to remain under guard for 26 months as a protection to swimmers, was returned to the custody of Fortune yesterday by the Rochester Dog Protective Association.*[202]

But, did life go back to normal for Victor and Idaho? A week's appearance in a local theater did not end the public's taste for more entertainment involving the Brockport "murder dog." An advertisement for the Loew's Theater displayed another featured part of Idaho's stage appearances.[203]

The *Killer-Dog*[204] advertisement is a bit deceiving. It is billed as if it is about Idaho and somehow figured into his trial. The film is an MGM production released in August 1936. It was produced and narrated by Pete Smith, who created over 150 short-subject films for MGM, and was directed by Jacques Tourneur, who a few years later directed classics like *Cat People* (1942), *Out of the Past* (1949) and *Stars in My Crown* (1950).[205] Short movie subjects in this era were part of the studios' exhibition packages, along with serials, animated cartoons, newsreels and travel documentaries.

Killer-Dog is a nine-minute short-subject film about a dog on trial for his life. However, this dog is accused of killing sheep (a similarity to the 1870 Old Drum trial). The owner defends the dog in court himself, much as Victor had to do in the hearing. Just when the circumstantial evidence seems assured of condemning the dog, he demands that the dog be able to defend himself, similar to Sessions's demand in Idaho's trial. The judge agrees, and the dog proves not to be the killer.[206] It does have parallels to Idaho's trial, with the requests to have the dog defend itself and the fact that both dogs were on trial for their lives.

Left: Rochester Lowe's Theater. *Reproduced by the author.*

Below: *Killer-Dog* theater advertisement. *Reproduced by the author.*

Killer-Dog trailer. *Reproduced by the author.*

One part of the advertisement for the film seems questionable. Would a judge view a "killer dog" film that is similar to the case he must decide, the day before he gives a decision in court? There is no doubt that the description of this film on the Loew's Theater advertisement is deceptive.

This film is further proof of how influential the Brockport trial was. It hardly seems a coincidence that a Hollywood short-subject film about a killer dog came out the same month as the Brockport trial, and little doubt remains when one considers that it was being promoted as the "premiere showing of a film in defence of 'Idaho', Brockport Killer Dog." It is doubtful that MGM bothered to send anyone to Brockport, because *Killer-Dog* is a different story that merely took advantage of the "murder dog" trial publicity. The theater advertisement suggests that the film was completed and shown to Judge Benedict before the trial. Of course, that would indicate the film was completed no later than August 4. The film is advertised in the August 7 Rochester *Democrat and Chronicle*. The official release date is August 26, 1936.[207] It also seems doubtful that Judge Benedict, who was quoted in the *Democrat and Chronicle* about his impartiality, would have viewed the film on August 4. "Justice Homer B.

Benedict, who will decide the case August 5, announced yesterday that despite the telegraphs and messages which he is receiving, counseling him as to what decision he should make, that 'public opinion will not influence me one way or the other.'"[208]

It seems that Judge Benedict was besieged by public opinion from all sides. First, there was the *Brockport Republic and Democrat* straw poll that was to be given to the judge over the objections of the defense attorney, Harry Sessions. Then there were the telegrams and letters. And finally, Hollywood was trying to influence him with a premiere of *Killer-Dog* on the evening before the verdict. Despite his assertion that public opinion would play no part in his ruling, the pressure was there.

Killer-Dog is entirely narrated and does not require the actors to learn any lines. It was also limited to two sets, so it is possible that it was produced and quickly released within the short period of time between the national publicity and sometime in August 1936. It was, however, not the only dog trial that made it to Hollywood. Remember the 1870 trial of Old Drum?

The 2000 movie *The Trial of Old Drum* has similarities to both the Brockport trial and the film *Killer-Dog*. *The Trial of Old Drum* is more like the "Killer-Dog" than the original 1870 trial. Old Drum is accused of killing sheep, exactly like "Killer-Dog," but Old Drum is not shot by a neighbor. He is put on trial. *The Trial of Old Drum* has the famous summation that ends with the line "a man's best friend is his dog." It is similar to the Brockport trial in one scene that seems to be taken directly from the trial's proceedings. Old Drum barks in response to a statement made in the courtroom, and the spectators laugh. This is reminiscent of the time in the Brockport trial when Idaho barked at Frank Morass's response of *"No!"* when asked if Idaho bites. The Brockport spectators also laughed.[209]

EVEN THOUGH IDAHO WAS saved from execution, his life was never the same after the trial. Everyone in the Fortune family kept a close eye on him, and Victor, who was employed, had little free time to spend with the dog. Idaho languished a great deal of time in the Fortune kitchen with Ada Fortune and was denied his love of swimming in the canal. Following the trial, a *New York Times* reporter described Idaho's situation as follows: "His owner lives in a dun-colored, six-room house, whose modest backyard is not exactly paradise as a dog's romping ground."[210]

Victor Fortune describes the circumstances surrounding Idaho's life after the trial.

Following the trial and return from Mary Foubister's, Idaho returned to our home at 306 Holley Street in Brockport. Destined to be tied to the chain for the next couple of years, Idaho's life was forever changed. No more swimming in the Erie Canal, no more running free chasing a ball.

Mom was great with Idaho most of the time following the trial. He would spend much time with her in the kitchen or following her around the house! When Mom was around Idaho and I was gone, Idaho rarely took his eyes off her because there might be an occasional treat! During the day when he was staked outside on the chain serving his sentence, Mom would garden, do laundry or sit on the porch to read. Mom was afraid to leave him outside alone fearing someone would come steal him or hurt him. Idaho's life was never the same, nor was Mom's. When she walked to town, some people continued to cross the street if they saw her. Once in a while people would say things like "Idaho should be dead" or point their finger and say, "that's the mother of Victor Fortune—the killer dog Idaho." That lasted for years. My Mother was the most sensitive about what was being said. Most of the time she didn't answer, she just walked away. Sometimes I'd hear her talking to Idaho saying, "You are an innocent dog—I know you didn't kill Maxie."

I now had a job at the cannery which turned into delivery of products to grocery stores and warehouses. I couldn't take Idaho with me like I did in the CCC's. Idaho stayed home with Mom. Jack would play with him and walk him every day after school, but there was no more swimming or running free except on weekends when we would occasionally drive to Canandaigua or somewhere outside Monroe County so Idaho could run. We didn't do that very often. Money was still tight and working was a privilege that you didn't take lightly. If you were asked to work extra hours, you worked and they were long days, many weekends especially when fresh harvest was brought in.

Idaho and I had our rituals. Mornings I would take him out and feed him. He was a great dog. When I came home he was all over me. He'd sit on my feet under the table during dinner and snuggle up at the end of my bed every night. When I was home, he was never far from me. Jack spent a lot of time with Idaho, but at night he was mine. Our life was a fairly normal routine for the times. The two years passed. Mary Foubister was still trying to get Idaho pardoned and was very excited when the pardon was granted.[211]

In 1938, only a few days before his sentence was up, Idaho was given a pardon by New York State Supreme Court justice William F. Love. Victor chose to keep Idaho confined for the remaining few days of his sentence.[212] However, even after the pardon and the confinement order was served, Victor worried about Idaho's safety and the effect that the years of confinement had on the dog and his ability to successfully cope with freedom.

Following Idaho's release, Jack was really excited to take Idaho muskrat trapping and hunting in the neighboring woods. Jack was now in his teens and was always asking to take Idaho off the chain or the leash. I continually told him no because Idaho had no fear of motor vehicles. Idaho would come when he was called but not always. If he had the scent of an animal, he would drag you on the leash and he dragged Jack plenty. I caught Jack a couple of times letting go of the lead so Idaho could run and follow the animal scent. Idaho was strong willed and would not always come back immediately.

Jack continued to work with Idaho without my knowledge. He believed Idaho would always obey. I knew better but I was older. The day Idaho was hit, Mom told him to make sure Idaho stayed on the leash. Jack smiled and he and Idaho went off to the woods like any other winter day. They would check the traps and follow animal tracks in the snow.

Jack was alone and Idaho was off leash. Suddenly he got the scent of a cat and began to chase the cat. Jack commanded him "back" and Idaho kept going, running in front of a car and was killed instantly. The car didn't stop, it just kept going. A neighbor saw it all and called the police and my mother. The neighbor's wife went to Jack. Jack was inconsolable. They moved Idaho from the road. My Mom now had to go to Jack. Both were heartbroken. The police brought them home.

When I came home from work and was told what happened, I cannot explain my grief. I was angry with Jack but I also felt compassion for him. If only he had listened. But, he was a "know it all" kid. My Mother and Jack wrapped Idaho in an old quilt that Idaho slept on at the foot of my bed. When I saw his limp and lifeless body, I could not speak. We buried Idaho together, as a family, behind our house under the stake that Idaho had been tied to for the last years.[213]

The Brockport "murder dog" trial continued to be news long after the trial was over. Few news items about canine "criminals" could resist mentioning Idaho and the Brockport trial. A Wilmington, Delaware newspaper ran a headline and story about a dog that attacked three cows in Newark, New York. The story began with the retelling of the Idaho trial.

Dog Arrested After Attack Upon 3 Cows. Western New York, where the trial of Brockport dog, Idaho, on a charge that he caused the drowning of a boy was held recently, looked with interest upon another canine prisoner today.[214]

Victor Fortune suffered much the same fate. He never could escape from being labeled as the owner of the "murder dog." Five years after the trial, when he and his brother Norman enlisted in the army during World War II, the 1941 headline read: "Idaho's Master Joins 209th for Service in Georgia." Almost every article about the 209th Artillery unit that mentioned Victor reminded readers that he was the former owner of the dog Idaho. This is an example of one of them: "They include Corp. Vic Fortune whom newspaper readers will recall as owner of the famous dog Idaho in the Brockport trial case."[215]

Ada Fortune soon had more to worry about. She now had three sons in the Pacific theater during World War II. Vic, Norm and Jack ended up with a total of ten years in the armed forces during the war. A newspaper article in 1945 reminded readers, nine years after the trial, that Victor Fortune was the owner of Idaho. For most of the rest of his life, the story followed him wherever he went.[216]

Victor Fortune would continue to confront the events that began on July 4, 1936. No matter where he went, even overseas, the Brockport trial was always there. "The story was always a part of me. When I joined the military and went overseas, guys would say to me, "You're the Victor Fortune who had the dog Idaho!' I would always smile and the story would come back as though it were yesterday. It didn't matter what part of the U.S. those guys came from; they knew the story."[217]

Even after the war, twelve years after the trial, the story followed Victor when he met the father of the woman he would marry. "In 1948, I met my wife, Betty Resch. She took me to her home to meet her father, Joe. The first thing he said, 'So you're the guy who had the dog Idaho. I followed your story! We gave pennies to the little girl down the street who was collecting for Idaho's defense!' And, as always, I was almost haunted by the thought of the Breezes, the feel of Idaho's fur and my mind raced back in time."[218]

Seventeen years elapsed, and in 1953, Victor was involved in a near-fatal accident when the truck he was in went down a seventy-five-foot ravine into a raging stream. The rescue of Victor and his companion was complicated by the depth of the embankment, the forest and high, fast-moving water. The news article could not resist informing its readers that one of the men in the accident was the owner of Idaho, the Brockport "murder dog."[219]

Left: Victor Fortune in uniform, World War II. *Right*: Victor Fortune and Betty Resch Fortune. *Author's collection.*

On the twenty-fifth anniversary of the Brockport trial, newspapers wanted to revive the story, and again Victor and his family had to relive the tragedy. Would this obsession with the trial ever end? "Just before July 4, 1961, the Rochester *Democrat and Chronicle* called me to review the events of 25 years before. They had called Mom and Dad. Once again, the topic was on the table and the events fresh in my mind."[220]

Victor had to wait eight more years, thirty-three years after the trial, when the Brockport Town Hall, the building in which the trial was held, was demolished and the story was being retold in the press one more time.

In 1969, when the Village Hall was torn down, the story of the famous dog murder trial was resurrected. I had spent hours remembering the time I spent in the office of Judge Benedict, the fear of losing Idaho, the flashing lights, the sadness. I also remembered the excitement of still having Idaho when the trial was over. Such a range of emotions.

This time it was different for me. I now had three young girls of my own and I simply couldn't bear the thought of anything ever happening to them. Laurie was about to start 4th grade, which is where my story began.

Above: Brockport Town Hall, circa 1930. *Reproduced by the author.*

Left: Paramount newsreel ending. *Reproduced by the author.*

However, the story that began in 1936 did not end. Victor could never have guessed what would happen on Laurie's first day in the fourth grade, which would open up the story to his daughters and granddaughters. Nor could he have imagined that fifty years after the trial his story would be performed to schoolchildren in the very place where he himself went to school.

POSTSCRIPT

About fifty years after the famous trial, the Arts for Children program at SUNY College at Brockport started to do research into local history events that might be adaptable to theater productions for children. This was when one of the authors, a professor in the theater department and the Arts for Children program, began his investigation of the circumstances surrounding the 1936 case with his students. The idea was to take these performances into schools to teach local history to children through drama. Dr. Joanna Kraus took the idea further by writing and publishing a children's play about the trial.

> *The Shaggy Dog Murder Trial (Playscript) by Joanna Halpert Kraus was awarded the Charlotte B. Chorpenning Playwright Award. It is a one-act, participatory, theatre-in-education play. Suitable for all ages, especially 4th to 7th grades. Simple interior set. Easy to tour. Cast of 5 men, 3 women. Approx. running time: 60 minutes.*
>
> *This one-act, participatory play is designed for a student audience of 4th through 7th graders. The script may also be used as a theatre-in-education vehicle. The dramatization is based on one of America's most unusual court cases, in which a mongrel dog is accused when a boy drowns. It results in a trial that receives nationwide coverage, splitting the town in half. The testimony of the witnesses is contradictory. It is up to the audience to vote whether the shaggy dog should live or die. A study guide is available in the script.*[221]

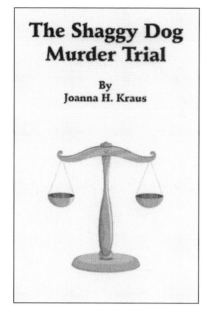

Left: Shaggy Dog *theater script. Right:* Letter to Laurie Verbridge from Joanna Kraus. *Author's collection.*

The play was performed on a tour of local schools by the College at Brockport Arts for Children students in the spring semester of 1986. Unfortunately, Joanna did not know that a principle character, whom she called Bixby Price in her play, was still alive and living locally. Laurie, his daughter and the coauthor of this book, heard from a friend in the college library about the play being staged. She called the college to talk with Joanna, but the semester was over and Joanna was not in. When Joanna finally received the message, she answered with the accompanying correspondence. This is how close the two authors of this book came to meeting in 1986. And, as this book proves, the story is still being retold eighty years later.

The story spread far and wide, all over America. Every newspaper printed long accounts of it. There were editorials pro and con. It was the most spectacular case involving a dog in the history of criminal law. The whole thing must constitute a mighty good dog story.[222]

—Albert Payson Terhune, syndicated columnist and author

APPENDIX 1

Cue Sheet from Paramount "Eyes and Ears of the World" Newsreel

The Paramount news crew filmed before, during and after the trial, capturing interviews with Anna and William Breeze, Victor Fortune, Mary Foubister, Daniel Houghton, Dr. William Mahoney and Judge Homer Benedict. They obtained shots of Idaho in his cage, being led into the courtroom and sleeping at the feet of Deputy Tuttle. They also filmed scenes from the canal where a young man swam in the water with Idaho. A brief description of the audio and film in the Paramount news clip follows. The nitrate film still exists in the Sherman Grinberg Film Library (21011 Itasca Street, Chatsworth, California, 91311), and the authors obtained a digital copy of the film from the Grinberg Film Library and the necessary rights to use quotes and still-frame photographs in this book.

Brockport, New York (reel 1)
*(visual) Dog on trial, charged with murder of boy.
*head cut of dog thru bars.
*general view of canal.
*semi view of 4 boys lying on grass. semi cut of 2 boys.
*top view of man taking dog in water.
*general view of man swimming. dog going towards him.
*cut of dog trying to get on man's back.
*general view of dog on man's back.
*semi view pose of mother and father seated on steps. (Mr. and Mrs. Breeze).

*semi cut of mother speaking. semi cut of father speaking.

*semi view of owner of dog speaking.

*semi view of judge speaking.

*general view of hutch and dog.

*semi cut of woman and dog.

*sound effects: off-stage voice: "This is Idaho charged with murder. They say he drowned 14-year-old Maxwell Breeze in the canal when he was swimming."

*friends of boy talk about dog. mother and father both speak and wish to have the dog killed.

*Victor Fortune, owner of dog, says: "I've owned this dog for 7 mos. and he wouldn't purposely drown a boy."

*Judge says: "I shall endeavor to decide whether or not Idaho is a dangerous dog or not. if so found, he will be shot or confined. if not dangerous he will be free."

*chairman of the Idaho defense funds speaks.

*dogs barking etc. noises.

Brockport, N.Y. (reel 2)

Title shot: Dog cleared of murder but gets two years.

*general view of court house.

*cut of dog int. view of dog arriving at court house.

*elevated pan int. v. of court room.

*cut of Judge Benedict.

*general view of reporter interview.

*head cut of boy witness.

*semi view of dog sleeping at feet of cop.

*semi cut of owner of dog.

*head cut of judge benedict reading sentence.

*general view of owner and defendant.

*sound effects: off-stage voice tells about mongrel dog named Idaho, accused of having drowned a 14 yr. old boy, and having trial.

*lawyer questioning witnesses.

*Judge says: "I've decided that the actions of the dog Idaho while in the water are dangerous and that subject to it is hereby ordered to securely confine that dog from this date of October 1928.

*var. gen. etc. noises.

APPENDIX 2

New York State Agriculture and Markets Law. Chapter 69. Of the Consolidated Laws. Article 7. Licensing, Identification and Control of Dogs. § 123. Dangerous dogs

1. Any person who witnesses an attack or threatened attack, or in the case of a minor, an adult acting on behalf of such minor, may make a complaint of an attack or threatened attack upon a person, companion animal as defined in section three hundred fifty of this chapter, farm animal as defined in such section three hundred fifty, or a domestic animal as defined in subdivision seven of section one hundred eight of this article, to a dog control officer or police officer of the appropriate municipality. Such officer shall immediately inform the complainant of his or her right to commence a proceeding as provided in subdivision two of this section and, if there is reason to believe the dog is a dangerous dog, the officer shall forthwith commence such proceeding himself or herself.

2. Any person who witnesses an attack or threatened attack, or in the case of a minor, an adult acting on behalf of such minor, may, and any dog control officer or police officer as provided in subdivision one of this section shall, make a complaint under oath or affirmation to any municipal judge or justice of such attack or threatened attack. Thereupon, the judge or justice shall immediately determine if there is probable cause to believe the dog is a dangerous dog and, if so, shall issue an order to any dog control officer, peace officer, acting pursuant to his or her special duties, or police officer directing such officer to immediately seize such dog and hold the same pending judicial determination as provided in this section. Whether or not the judge or justice finds there is probable cause for such seizure, he or she shall, within

five days and upon written notice of not less than two days to the owner of the dog, hold a hearing on the complaint. The petitioner shall have the burden at such hearing to prove the dog is a "dangerous dog" by clear and convincing evidence. If satisfied that the dog is a dangerous dog, the judge or justice shall then order neutering or spaying of the dog, microchipping of the dog and one or more of the following as deemed appropriate under the circumstances and as deemed necessary for the protection of the public: (a) evaluation of the dog by a certified applied behaviorist, a board-certified veterinary behaviorist, or another recognized expert in the field and completion of training or other treatment as deemed appropriate by such expert. The owner of the dog shall be responsible for all costs associated with evaluations and training ordered under this section;

(b) secure, humane confinement of the dog for a period of time and in a manner deemed appropriate by the court but in all instances in a manner designed to: (1) prevent escape of the dog, (2) protect the public from unauthorized contact with the dog, and (3) to protect the dog from the elements pursuant to section three hundred fifty-three-b of this chapter. Such confinement shall not include lengthy periods of tying or chaining;

(c) restraint of the dog on a leash by an adult of at least twenty-one years of age whenever the dog is on public premises;

(d) muzzling the dog whenever it is on public premises in a manner that will prevent it from biting any person or animal, but that shall not injure the dog or interfere with its vision or respiration; or

(e) maintenance of a liability insurance policy in an amount determined by the court, but in no event in excess of one hundred thousand dollars for personal injury or death resulting from an attack by such dangerous dog.

3. Upon a finding that a dog is dangerous, the judge or justice may order humane euthanasia or permanent confinement of the dog if one of the following aggravating circumstances is established at the judicial hearing held pursuant to subdivision two of this section:

(a) the dog, without justification, attacked a person causing serious physical injury or death; or

(b) the dog has a known vicious propensity as evidenced by a previous unjustified attack on a person, which caused serious physical injury or death; or

(c) the dog, without justification, caused serious physical injury or death to a companion animal, farm animal or domestic animal, and has, in the past two years, caused unjustified physical injury or death to a companion or farm animal as evidenced by a "dangerous dog" finding pursuant to the provisions of this section. An order of humane euthanasia shall not be carried out until expiration of the thirty day period provided for in subdivision five of this section for filing a notice of appeal, unless the owner of the dog has indicated to the judge in writing, his or her intention to waive his or her right to appeal. Upon filing of a notice of appeal, the order shall be automatically stayed pending the outcome of the appeal.

4. A dog shall not be declared dangerous if the court determines the conduct of the dog (a) was justified because the threat, injury or damage was sustained by a person who at the time was committing a crime or offense upon the owner or custodian of the dog or upon the property of the owner or custodian of the dog; (b) was justified because the injured, threatened or killed person was tormenting, abusing, assaulting or physically threatening the dog or its offspring, or has in the past tormented, abused, assaulted or physically threatened the dog or its offspring; (c) was justified because the dog was responding to pain or injury, or was protecting itself, its owner, custodian, or a member of its household, its kennels or its offspring; or was justified because the injured, threatened or killed companion animal, farm animal or domestic animal was attacking or threatening to attack the dog or its offspring. Testimony of a certified applied behaviorist, a board-certified veterinary behaviorist, or another recognized expert shall be relevant to the court's determination as to whether the dog's behavior was justified pursuant to the provisions of this subdivision.

5. (a) The owner of a dog found to be a "dangerous dog" pursuant to this section may appeal such determination, and/or the court's order concerning disposition of the dog to the court having jurisdiction to hear civil appeals in the county where the "dangerous dog" finding was made. The owner shall commence such appeal by filing a notice of appeal with the appropriate court within thirty days of the final order pursuant to this section. Court rules governing civil appeals in the appropriate jurisdiction shall govern the appeal of a determination under this section.

(b) Upon filing a notice of appeal from an order of humane euthanasia pursuant to this section, such order shall be automatically stayed pending final determination of any appeal. In all other circumstances, the owner of the dog may make application to the court to issue a stay of disposition pending determination of the appeal.

6. The owner of a dog who, through any act or omission, negligently permits his or her dog to bite a person, service dog, guide dog or hearing dog causing physical injury shall be subject to a civil penalty not to exceed four hundred dollars in addition to any other applicable penalties.

7. The owner of a dog who, through any act or omission, negligently permits his or her dog to bite a person causing serious physical injury shall be subject to a civil penalty not to exceed one thousand five hundred dollars in addition to any other applicable penalties. Any such penalty may be reduced by any amount which is paid as restitution by the owner of the dog to the person or persons suffering serious physical injury as compensation for unreimbursed medical expenses, lost earnings and other damages resulting from such injury.

8. The owner of a dog who, through any act or omission, negligently permits his or her dog, which had previously been determined to be dangerous pursuant to this article, to bite a person causing serious physical injury, shall be guilty of a misdemeanor punishable by a fine of not more than three thousand dollars, or by a period of imprisonment not to exceed ninety days, or by both such fine and imprisonment in addition to any other applicable penalties. Any such fine may be reduced by any amount which is paid as restitution by the owner of the dog to the person or persons suffering serious physical injury as compensation for unreimbursed medical expenses, lost earnings and other damages resulting from such injury.

9. If any dog, which had previously been determined by a judge or justice to be a dangerous dog, as defined in section one hundred eight of this article, shall without justification kill or cause the death of any person who is peaceably conducting himself or herself in any place where he or she may lawfully be, regardless of whether such dog escapes without fault of the owner, the owner shall be guilty of a class A misdemeanor in addition to any other penalties.

10. The owner or lawful custodian of a dangerous dog shall, except in the circumstances enumerated in subdivisions four and eleven of this section, be strictly liable for medical costs resulting from injury caused by such dog to a person, companion animal, farm animal or domestic animal.

11. The owner shall not be liable pursuant to subdivision six, seven, eight, nine or ten of this section if the dog was coming to the aid or defense of a person during the commission or attempted commission of a murder, robbery, burglary, arson, rape in the first degree as defined in subdivision one or two of section 130.35 of the penal law, criminal sexual act in the first degree as defined in subdivision one or two of section 130.50 of the penal law or kidnapping within the dwelling or upon the real property of the owner of the dog and the dog injured or killed the person committing such criminal activity.

12. Nothing contained in this section shall limit or abrogate any claim or cause of action any person who is injured by a dog with a vicious disposition or a vicious propensity may have under common law or by statute. The provisions of this section shall be in addition to such common law and statutory remedies.

13. Nothing contained in this section shall restrict the rights and powers derived from the provisions of title four of article twenty-one of the public health law relating to rabies and any rule and regulation adopted pursuant thereto.

14. Persons owning, possessing or harboring dangerous dogs shall report the presence of such dangerous dogs pursuant to section two hundred nine-cc of the general municipal law.

APPENDIX 3

Court Summons for Hearing

Left: Summons (part 1). *Right*: Summons (part 2). *Author's collection*.

NOTES

Chapter 1

1. "Pup's Fate in Trial Divides Brockport," *New York Times*.
2. Merrill, *Changing Years*, 161.
3. Silverman, "Dog Day in Court," *Useless Information*.
4. Terhune, "Tales of Real Dogs," *Montgomery Advertiser*.
5. Kraus, *Shaggy Dog Murder Trial*.
6. Terhune, *Asbury Park Press*, July 3, 1939, 3.
7. Kraus, *Shaggy Dog Murder Trial*.
8. Terhune, "Tales of Real Dogs," *Montgomery Advertiser*.
9. "Baseball Gets Thrilling Start," *Brockport Republic-Democrat*.
10. Ibid.
11. Schafer, "Idaho Dog Trial," 1.
12. Ibid., 1.
13. "Rakers Lead Softball League," *Brockport Republic-Democrat*.
14. "Dog on Trial as Slayer Spared, to Be Confined," *Chicago Tribune*.
15. Victor Fortune, interviews with coauthor Laurie Fortune Verbridge, September 1961–95.
16. Ibid.
17. Ibid.
18. "Works Progress Administration," History.com, www.history.com/topics/great-depression/works-progress-administration.
19. "Boy Scouts Receive Many Awards at Honor Court," *Brockport Republic and Democrat*, April 11, 1935, 1.

20. Ibid.
21. Ibid.

Chapter 2

22. Fortune, interviews.
23. Bracker, "Pup Gets 2 Years in Boy's Drowning," *New York Times*.
24. Ibid.
25. Ibid.
26. "Master Hides Dog Facing Murder Trial," *Elmira Star Gazette*, July 21, 1936.
27. Ibid.
28. Fortune, interviews.
29. Schafer, "Idaho Dog Trial," 3.
30. See Appendix 2: New York State Agriculture and Markets Law. Chapter 69. Of the Consolidated Laws Article 7. Licensing, Identification and Control of Dogs.
31. See Appendix 3: Justice Court Civil Docket. State of New York, County of Monroe, Justice Court–Town of Sweden.

Chapter 3

32. Fortune, interviews.
33. "Condemned Dog Is to Receive Chance of Self Defense," *Tyler Morning Telegraph*.
34. "Court Decides Accused Dog Fate Aug. 5," *Democrat and Chronicle*.
35. "Pleas and Protests on Pup Flow to Brockport Judge," *Democrat and Chronicle*.
36. "Court Decides Aug. 5," 17.
37. Terhune, *True Dog Stories*.
38. Terhune, "Tales of Real Dogs," 26.
39. Ibid.
40. Ibid.
41. "Court Decides Accused Dog Fate Aug. 5," *Democrat and Chronicle*.
42. "Pleas and Protests on Pup Flow to Brockport Judge," *Democrat and Chronicle*.
43. Ibid.
44. Ibid.
45. "Children's Pennies to Defend Idaho," *Democrat and Chronicle*.
46. Ibid.
47. "Court Decides Accused Dog Fate Aug. 5," *Democrat and Chronicle*.
48. Ibid.

49. Henry W. Clune, "Seen and Heard," *Democrat and Chronicle.*

50. "Idaho Given Parole Term," *Poughkeepsie, Eagle-News.*

51. "Master Hides Dog Facing Murder Trial," *Elmira Star Gazette.*

52. "Pup's Fate in Trial."

53. Ibid.

54. Charles A. Smith, letter dated July 31, 1936, from the collection of Victor Fortune.

55. Fortune, interviews.

56. "Many Letters Appeal to Save Idaho From Death," *Brockport Republic and Democrat.*

57. "Alibi Dog to Be Produced at Trial to Save Idaho's Life," *Democrat and Chronicle.*

58. "383 Votes Cast in R-D Idaho Poll," *Brockport Republic and Democrat,* August 6, 1936.

Chapter 4

59. Merrill, *Changing Years,* 161.

60. Ibid.

61. Douglas Linder, "Trial Account," www.Law2.umkc.edu/projects/ Hauptmann/Hauptmann.htl.

62. "State vs. Dog," *Bangor Daily News,* 6.

63. McNamara, "Curiosities of the Law: Animal Prisoner at the Bar," *Notre Dame Law,* 32.

64. Jen Girgin, "The Historical and Contemporary Prosecution and Punishment of Animals," *Animal Law* 9 (2003): 106.

65. Shakespeare, *Merchant of Venice,* 68.

66. Evans, *Criminal Prosecution and Capital Punishment of Animals,* 334.

67. Ibid., 329–34.

68. Witz and Hlawon, "On Racine's the Litigants," *Oñati Socio-Legal Series.*

69. Evans, *Criminal Prosecution,* 167.

70. Hugo, *Hunchback of Notre Dame.*

71. Ibid., 154.

72. Ibid., 158.

73. McWilliams, "Beastly Justice," *Slate.*

74. Long, *Trial of farmer Carter's dog, Porter, for murder.*

75. McWilliams, "Beastly Justice."

76. "Drowned Boy's Mother Bitter as Court Spares Life of a Dog," *Tribune,* 2.

77. McWilliams, "Beastly Justice."

78. *Holy Bible,* 2–3.

79. Evans, *Criminal Prosecution,* 344.

80. Ibid., 313–34.

81. Merrill, *Changing Years*, 161.

82. Katie Sykes, "Human Drama, Animal Trials: What the Medieval Animal Trials Can Teach Us about Justice for Animals," Animal Legal and Historical Center, https://www.animallaw.info/sites/default/files/lralvol17_2_273.pdf.

83. Bracker, "Pup Gets 2 Years," 1.

84. "Courtroom Crowd Roars Approval as Judge Spares Idaho's Life in Drowning Trial," *Democrat and Chronicle*, 15.

85. "Alibi Dog."

86. Terhune, "Tales of Real Dogs," 26.

87. "Pup's Fate in Trial."

88. Ibid.

89. Witz and Hlawon, "On Racine's the Litigants," 1150.

90. Justice Court Civil Document, State of New York, County of Monroe. Authors' italics.

91. Fortune, interviews.

Chapter 5

92. Paramount newsreel.

93. Ibid.

94. Ibid.

95. Ibid.

96. Ibid.

97. Fortune, interviews.

98. Ibid.

99. Bracker, "Pup Gets 2 Years," 8.

100. See Appendix 2: New York State Agriculture and Markets Law. Chapter 69. Of the Consolidated Laws. Article 7. Licensing, Identification and Control of Dogs.

101. "Pup on Trial For Life Snores While Witnesses Testify," *Daily Times*.

102. Bracker, "Pup Gets 2 Years," 8.

103. Ibid.

104. Ibid.

105. Victor Fortune, interviews.

106. Ibid.

107. Ibid.

108. Bracker, "Pup Gets 2 Years," 8.

Chapter 6

109. "Pup On Trial For Life Snores While Witnesses Testify," *Daily Times*.
110. "Spares Life of Dog Held in Drowning Boy," *Intelligencer Journal*, August 3, 1936, 3.
111. "Drowning Case Dog Stirs New Cop Controversy," *Wilkes-Barre Times Leader*.
112. Ibid.
113. Ibid.
114. "Hero Dog Sends Dollar Gift to Defense Fund for Idaho," *Democrat and Chronicle*.
115. Ibid.
116. "Idaho Cleared, Crowd Cheers," *Democrat and Chronicle*.

Chapter 7

117. "Kidnapping and Trial," Minnesota Historical Society.
118. Ibid.
119. Ibid.
120. Ibid.
121. Fortune, interviews.
122. Ibid.
123. Ibid.
124. "Civilian Conservation Corps," History.com.
125. Ada Fortune, letter to Victor Fortune, September 21, 1933.
126. Visit Ithaca, www.vistithaca.com.
127. Fortune, interviews.
128. Ibid.
129. I Love New York.
130. "Works Progress Administration."
131. Ibid.
132. Ibid.
133. "Boy Scouts Receive Many Awards at Honor Court."
134. "Local, Chain Radio Programs Scheduled for Broadcast Today," *Democrat and Chronicle*, April 28, 1936, 24.
135. Merrill, *Changing Years*, 161.
136. Ibid.

Chapter 8

137. Merrill, 161.
138. "Reporter Swims with Killer Dog," *Times Herald.*
139. Ibid.
140. Ibid.
141. Ibid.
142. "Dog Defendant in Court Again," *Democrat and Chronicle*, 17.
143. "Dog Trial," *Lancaster New Era*, 3.
144. "Idaho Released During Good Behavior Next Two Years," *Brockport Republic and Democrat*, August 6, 1936, 4.
145. "Dog Defendant In Court Again."
146. Terhune, "Tales of Real Dogs," 26.
147. Silverman, "Dog Day in Court," *Useless Information.*
148. Ibid.
149. "Idaho Cleared, Crowd Cheers."

Chapter 9

150. "Crowd Cheers When Magistrate Spares Life Of Mongrel Canine," *Daily Messenger.*
151. "Idaho Given Parole Term," *Poughkeepsie Eagle-News.*
152. Fortune, interviews.
153. Fortune.
154. "Alibi Dog May Deliver Mongrel from Execution on Murder Charge," *Intelligencer Journal.*
155. Silverman, "Dog Day in Court."
156. Ibid.
157. "Idaho Not Guilty," *Morning News.*
158. "Courtroom Crowd Roars Approval," *Democrat and Chronicle.*
159. Coren, "Landmark Case for the Legal Rights of Dogs?" *Psychology Today.*
160. Fortune, interviews.
161. Ibid.
162. Ibid.
163. "Dog on Trial Charged with Murder of Boy," Paramount newsreel.
164. Fortune, interviews.

Chapter 10

165. "Dogs in the Slammer," *ABA Journal*.

166. Girgin, "Historical and Contemporary Prosecution," 122–23.

167. Ibid., 124–25.

168. Jane Briggs-Bunting, "Judged a Vicious Canine, Champion Show Dog King Boots Must Lose His Life or His Bite," *People* 23, no. 5 (1984), https://people.com.

169. Ibid.

170. Ibid.

171. Ibid.

172. Ibid.

173. "Dogs in the Slammer."

174. Malcolm Gladwell, "The Howl of the Doomed," *Washington Post*, July 26, 1993.

175. Ibid.

176. Girgin, "Historical and Contemporary Prosecution," 124.

177. Gladwell. "Howl of the Doomed."

178. Ibid.

179. Ibid.

180. Kate Stone Lombardi, "Pardoned in Jersey, Taro Incognito," *New York Times*, March 20, 1994, 13.

181. Girgin, "Historical and Contemporary Prosecution," 124–25.

182. Ibid., 126–27.

183. "Magistrate Spares Dog's Life in Trial for Drowning Boy," *Baltimore Sun*.

184. Moore, "Dog that Stood Trial for Murder," *Crime Magazine*.

185. Ibid.

186. "Ye Towne Gossip," *Washington Times*, ed-1.

187. Ibid.

188. Phil Edwards@PhilEdwardsIncphil.

189. Moore, "Dog that Stood Trial."

190. Bracker, "Pup Gets 2 Years," 8.

191. Coren, "Landmark Case for the Legal Rights."

192. Ibid.

193. Ibid.

194. Edwards@PhilEdwardsInc.

195. Coren, "'Man's Best Friend'."

196. Ibid.

197. "'Eulogy' to Old Drum," Warrensburg Convention & Visitors Bureau.

198. Bracker, "Pup Gets 2 Years," 8.

199. Silverman, "Dog Day in Court."

Epilogue

200. Fortune.
201. "Dog May Get Chance in Films" *Ithaca Journal.*
202. Fortune.
203. Ibid.
204. "Killer Dog," *Democrat and Chronicle.*
205. Ibid.
206. Ibid.
207. Ibid.
208. "Defense Fund Begun By Girl to Save Dog," *Democrat and Chronicle.*
209. "Trial of Old Drum," Internet Movie Database.
210. Bracker, "Pup Gets 2 Years," 1.
211. Victor Fortune, interviews.
212. "Dog Ends Its Term For 1936 Drowning," *New York Times.*
213. Fortune, interviews.
214. "Dog Arrested After Attack on 3 Cows," *News Journal.*
215. "209th's Guns Boom along South Coast," *Democrat and Chronicle.*
216. Ibid.
217. Fortune, interviews.
218. Ibid.
219. Ibid.
220. Ibid.

Postscript

221. Kraus, Shaggy Dog Murder Trial.
222. Terhune, "Tales of Real Dogs," 26.

BIBLIOGRAPHY

Baltimore Sun. "Magistrate Spares Dog's Life in Trial for Drowning Boy." August 6, 1936, 3.

Bangor (ME) Daily News. "State vs. Dog." August 11, 1936, 6.

Bracker, Milton. "Pup Gets 2 Years in Boy's Drowning." *New York Times*, August 6, 1936.

Brockport (NY) Republic-Democrat. "Baseball Gets Thrilling Start." April 16, 1936, 1.

———. "Law Cleric Will Be Justice of Sweden." December 30, 1937, 1.

———. "Rakers Lead Softball League." June 25, 1936, 1.

Chicago Tribune. "Dog on Trial as Slayer Spared, to Be Confined." August 6, 1936, 10.

Clune, Henry. "Seen and Heard." *Democrat and Chronicle* (Rochester, NY), July 26, 1936, 18.

Cohen, Esther. "Law, Folklore and Animal Lore." *Past and Present* 110, issue 1, 1986. 6–37.

Coren, Stanley. "A Landmark Case for the Legal Rights of Dogs?" *Psychology Today* (March 11, 2015).

———. "'Man's Best Friend': The Senator, the Dog, and the Trial." *Psychology Today* (October 21, 2009).

"Court Spares Dog's Life." *Cincinnati Inquirer*, August 6, 1936, 1.

Daily Messenger (Hagerstown, MD). "Crowd Cheers When Magistrate Spares Life of Mongrel Canine." August 6, 1936, 4.

Daily Times (Davenport, IA). "Pup on Trial for Life Snores While Witnesses Testify." August 5, 1936, 1.

Davis, Frank C. *My C.C.C. Days.* Boone, NC: Parkways Publishers, 2006.

Democrat and Chronicle (Rochester, NY). "Children's Pennies to Defend Idaho." July 26, 1936, 18.

———. "Court Decides Accused Dog Fate Aug. 5." July 22, 1936, 17.

———. "Courtroom Crowd Roars Approval as Judge Spares Idaho's Life in Drowning Trial." August 6, 1936, 15.

———. "Defense Fund Begun by Girl to Save Dog." July 24, 1936, 17.

———. "Dog Defendant in Court Again." August 6, 1936, 17.

———. "Hero Dog Sends Dollar Gift to Defense Fund for Idaho." July 30, 1936.

———. "Idaho Cleared, Crowd Cheers." August 6, 1936, 17.

———. "The Killer Dog." August 7, 1936, 12.

———. "Strand Theater Has Entertained Generations." November 2, 2014.

———. "209th's Guns Boom along South Coast." May 5, 1941, 12.

"Dog on Trial Charged with Murder of Boy." Paramount newsreel, 1936.

"Dogs in the Slammer: Canines Get Tough Sentences." *ABA Journal* 36 (May 1985), 71.

Elmira (NY) Star Gazette. "Master Hides Dog Facing Murder Trial." July 21, 1936.

Evans, Edward Payson. *The Criminal Prosecution and Capital Punishment of Animals.* London: William Heinemann, 1906.

Fortune, Ada. Letter to Victor Fortune. September 21, 1933.

Fortune Verbridge, Laurie. Interviews with her father. September 1961–95.

History.com. "Civilian Conservation Corps." Accessed April 19, 2020. www.history.com.

The Holy Bible. Philadelphia, PA: Westminster Press, 1943.

Hugo, Victor. *The Hunchback of Notre Dame.* Translated by Walter J. Cobb. New York: Signet Classic, 1965 (1833).

I Love New York. www.iloveny.com.

Intelligencer Journal (Lancaster, PA). "Alibi Dog May Deliver Mongrel from Execution on Murder Charge." August 3, 1936, 2.

Internet Movie Database. "The Trial of Old Drum." www.imdb.com. 2000.

Ithaca (NY) Journal. "Dog May Get Chance in Films." August 7, 1936, 13.

Justice Court Civil Docket. State of New York, County of Monroe. Justice Court—Town of Sweden.

"Kidnapping and Trial." Minnesota Historical Society. https://www.mnhs.org.

Kraus, Joanna Halpert. *The Shaggy Dog Murder Trial.* New Orleans, LA: Anchorage Press, 1988.

Lancaster (PA) New Era. "Dog Trial." August 5, 1936, 3.

Long, Edward. *The trial of farmer Carter's dog, Porter, for Murder.* London: printed for T. Lowndes, 1771.

McNamara, Joseph P. "Curiosities of the Law: Animal Prisoner at the Bar." *Notre Dame Law* 30 (1927).

McWilliams, James. "Beastly Justice." *Slate.* February 21, 2013. https://slate.com.

Merrill, Arch. *The Changing Years.* New York: American Book Stratford Press, 1967.

Moore, Nolan. "The Dog That Stood Trial for Murder." *Crime Magazine* (March 21, 2016).

Morning News (Wilmington, DE). "Idaho Not Guilty." August 7, 1936, 8.

News Journal (Wilmington, DE). "Dog Arrested After Attack on 3 Cows." August 26, 1936, 7.

New York State Agriculture and Markets Law. Chapter 69. *Of the Consolidated Laws.* Article 7. "Licensing, Identification and Control of Dogs."

New York Times. "Dog Ends Its Term for 1936 Drowning." September 20, 1938, 7.

———. "Pup's Fate in Trial Divides Brockport." August 5, 1936, 21.

PhilEdwards@PhilEdwardsInc, phil.edwards@vox.com, March 4, 2015, 8:00 a.m. EST.

Poughkeepsie (NY) Eagle-News. "Idaho Given Parole Term." August 6, 1936, 2.

Schafer, Phyllis. "The Idaho Dog Trial." Unpublished manuscript. Brockport Library Seymour Library, Local History file, 1.

Shakespeare, William. *The Merchant of Venice.* Boston: Allyn and Bacon, 1896, 68.

Silverman, Steve. "A Dog Day in Court." *Useless Information* (podcast). Air date, March 31, 2016.

Terhune, Albert Payson. *Asbury Park (NJ) Press*, July 3, 1939, 3.

———. "Tales of Real Dogs." *Montgomery (AL) Advertiser*, March 21, 1937, 26.

———. *True Dog Stories.* New York: Saalfield Publishing Company, 1936.

Times Herald (Olean, NY). "Reporter Swims with Killer Dog." July 23, 1936, 7.

Tribune (Scranton, PA). "Drowned Boy's Mother Bitter as Court Spares Life of Dog." August 6, 1936, 2.

Tyler (TX) Morning Telegraph. "Condemned Dog Is to Receive Chance of Self Defense." July 31, 1936.

Warrensburg Convention & Visitors Bureau. "'Eulogy' to Old Drum." https://www.warrensburg-mo.com.

Washington Times. "Ye Towne Gossip." January 21, 1922, ed-1.

Wilkes-Barre (PA) Times Leader, Evening News. "Drowning Case Dog Stirs New Controversy." July 30, 1936, 1.

Witz, Claude, and Martin Hlawon. "On Racine's the Litigants." *Oñati Socio-Legal Series* 4, no. 6 (2014). Available at SSRN. https://ssrn.com/abstract=2543495.

INDEX

ABOUT THE AUTHORS

Photo by Jim Dusen.

Bill Hullfish is professor emeritus, SUNY College at Brockport. Toured under a grant from the National Endowment for the Arts and received a fellowship from the National Endowment for the Humanities. Member of the Clarkson Historical Society, the American Canal Society and the Canal Society of New York. Bill has written a number of books. His latest, *The Erie Canal Sings*, was published by The History Press. His articles have been published in *American Canals*, *Bottoming Out*, *Divisions*, *American Recorder*, *The Instrumentalist*, *New Jersey Outdoors* and *Bicycling*.

Laurie Fortune Verbridge is retired from K.M. Davies Company, Williamson, New York. She has held positions as the secretary for the Office of Public Information, Cornell University; postmaster, Pultneyville, New York; and postal service positions, including quality first facilitator, secretary human resources and rural letter carrier.

She is a member of the Williamson-Pultneyville Historical Society and Save Our Sodus Bay, is a past-president/trustee of the Williamson Central School Board of

Education and a past-president and state secretary of the Wayne County and State of New York Rural Letter Carriers.

Laurie has written letters to the editor of the *Williamson Sun and Record* and the *Times* of Wayne County, and she has formatted and written articles for "What's Happening" for Williamson Central School Board.

Visit us at
www.historypress.com
··